Viking Patterns for Knitting

ELSEBETH LAVOLD

Viking Patterns for Knitting
Inspiration and Projects for Today's Knitter

Photos by Per Erik Berglund

Translated by Robin Orm Hansen

Trafalgar Square Publishing

North Pomfret, Vermont

The frontispiece shows an ornamental metal plate from the Viking era, found in Solberga, Östergötland, Sweden

First published in the United States of America in 2000
by Trafalgar Square Publishing, North Pomfret, Vermont 05053

Photos: Per Erik Berglund: all garments; other photos, see p. 124.

Drawings and diagrams: p. 50 Sahlin 1904; others by Elsebeth Lavold.

Graphic design: Anders Rydell, Ingen Konst AB

ISBN-13: 978-1-57076-137-9

ISBN-10: 1-57076-137-X

Library of Congress Catalog Card Number: 99-65359

Printed in China

10 9 8 7 6

CONTENTS

Foreword

Few handcrafts can create such sophisticated products with such simple tools. All that's needed is a pair of knitting needles and a little yarn. From that simple beginning, the only limits are skill and imagination. Knitting occupies the hands but frees the mind.

I present this book with great pride, for many reasons.

First is the joy of bringing a part of my cultural heritage, the patterns of the Viking era, to life in a new context. After a full five years in close company with dragons and interlaced patterns, my fascination is, if possible, even greater than when I started, and to be able to reveal these wonderful, thousand-year-old patterns and show that they are still relevant, is genuine happiness. Second, I am able to share a technical innovation; partly because it shows that there are still things waiting to be discovered in knitting technology, and partly because I can now pass the baton to other knitters and designers. I hope they can use the technique to create new patterns with different premises and departure points.

I hope too that my systematic presentation will encourage others to develop further their own knowledge. One reason that knitting has been considered no more than a hobby, or therapy, the sort of thing one does when one has nothing better to do, is that entirely too few knitters and designers have engaged in systematic research and shared their results. I believe too that technical knowledge adds most and inspires best in an æsthetic context, when the designer shows how the technique has enriched her expression.

Finally, it's fun to show my designs with the hope that they will inspire knitting, design, and new discoveries in the wonderful world of knitting.

A project of this magnitude is never produced alone. I would first like to thank my four expert knitters, Helena Franzén, Irma Hansen, Gullevi Ljungström, and Brita Löwenadler. Their skill and knowledge have been invaluable, both in knitting the garments and correcting the directions and charts. Any remaining errors are mine, not theirs.

Many thanks to Per Erik Berglund, who was successful in changing my vague ideas on mood and atmosphere into beautiful photographs.

Thanks also to Stina Larsson, Thorleif and Josefin Lavold, Carina Lövman, and Sara Vretborn, who in weather ranging from 90° heat to bitter fall cold modeled my sweaters for the photographer.

For help with copy editing, I am grateful to my mother, Birgit Lavold, and for knit-technical editing of all the directions, to Helena Franzén.

Even before the project was completed, my yarn supplier generously donated yarn to knit the sample garments. Without this support the project would scarcely have been economically feasible. The many archeologists and the staff people of museums who helped me in my hunt for sources and information have also been an invaluable support.

Finally, I would like to thank my work/life/playmate Anders Rydell.

He gave the book form and took responsibility for putting all the pieces of the puzzle—the text and directions, the photos, the charts and drawings—not only in the right place but where they would best support one another. He has given my occasionally stiff texts a softer tone, added to my descriptions when my verbal inspiration dried up, and he wrote all the captions for the illustrations. He was at all the photo sessions, helped to choose the photos, and he has been my computer guru. He has supported and encouraged me, has been sounding board and critic. Without him, this book would not have been possible. It is almost as much his book as mine.

Spånga, November 1997
Elsebeth Lavold

A Project is Born

I can't say exactly when it first occurred to me to borrow the floral patterns of the Viking era. I just did it. Now, many years later, I have only scraped the surface of the enormous cultural treasure contained in everything from tiny metal plates to heavy rune stones. Many sweaters have come out of it. It became quite a project.

There are no archeological finds to prove that knitting was known or used during the Viking period. This *could* be because textiles, including knitting, are so perishable, but it's more likely that the Vikings, quite simply, didn't knit. The very same people who plaited the most fantastic patterns in silver thread a thousand years ago, would have been puzzled by the idea of looping yarn around a pair of knitting needles.

I first took up knitting seriously when I was in high school. I possessed the most elementary skills from those hateful home arts classes in school—knit and purl, cast on, bind off, increase and decrease—enough to begin knitting on my own. This led gradually to knitting, or actually to knitting design, as a choice of profession.

During the twenty years I have been active as a knitting designer, the emphasis in my design has shifted from color patterns to structural patterns. Besides their many possibilities for exciting textures, structural techniques have limitations that challenge me.

For the last fifteen years, I have collected patterns to try to discover and learn all known knitting techniques—as well as some unknown ones.

Plaited patterns have always had a special place in my heart, partly because of their strong graphic effect, partly because, once one gets used to crossing stitches, they are so easy to knit. Everything happens on the front side of the work, so you can always see what you're doing, and it's easy to see which stitches should be knitted and which purled.

It was when I coupled my long-term interest in archeology, especially the iron age and the Viking period, with my passion for braided patterns that my project began. In the beginning, it wasn't a project at all, just a few sweaters and the seed of an idea.

Aran patterns and other well-known braided patterns, cabling, in-

Tombstone from Hellvi, Gotland

terlace, and entre-lac are descriptions of the most typical patterns of the Viking period, that is, strips of knitting which in various ways are braided over, under, and around one another. Often animals twine around themselves in plaitwork including animals so stylized that their origin is hardly identifiable, but just as often it is simple strips that are interwoven.

The classic Aran patterns we know contain a number of braided patterns also found in objects from the Viking era. Here began my experiments.

Characteristically, the Aran braids consist of a number of stockinette knit strips of stitches which begin at the bottom and continue to the top of the garment, weaving over and under one another variously on the way. What would happen if one began to move the braids differently?

I experimented with changing the traditional interwoven patterns and hit on a few with a Viking feel to them. But the new variations soon became very much alike and I felt a desire to go on.

Now the hunt began for a source of patterns. In books and in museums I looked for patterns that could be adapted to knitting. I soon discovered that many were too complicated to adapt directly mainly because some of the elements of the braid change direction (vertically) smack in the middle of the pattern. Some also had motifs with beginnings and ends, that is, the elements of the braid were not continuous as in Aran interwoven patterns.

Viking Patterns and the New Technique

Some years earlier, I had taught myself to increase by knitting into the purl side of the stitch *under* the next stitch. Suddenly: insight! *Then, one must be able to do the opposite: knit a stitch and then increase by knitting in the purl side of the stitch beneath the one just knitted.* In this way, one could both have mirror image increases and have them right next to each other without making a hole in the work.

Using this technique, it was then possible to make motifs that began in the middle of a purled section without pulling up the base of the pattern. At the top, I could make mirror-image decreases and thereby get an attractive finish to the motif. By placing increases and decreases at different points relative to the knit stitches, I could get the strip to change direction vertically.

I began applying my new technique to old patterns, by adding a "start" and a "finish," making it possible to start and end patterns in the middle of the work. I also tried to work various patterns based on the traditional braided patterns.

Then, I sat down with the Viking period examples, a pen, graph paper, yarn, and knitting needles, to sort out where the boundaries of the possible lay. The next step was hands-on experimentation: draw, knit, change, draw and knit again. I found that if I placed a mirror image above a pattern panel, it gave a different impression.

One experiment followed another, and the collection of swatches grew. Variants of both Viking period ornamentation and my own new patterns came out of this, sometimes systematically, other times as the result of sudden inspiration.

The Viking Patterns Knitting Project

This was the point at which it became a project. There I sat with a bunch of sweaters, a bunch of patterns, a cultural heritage, a technical innovation, and a passion to share it all.

The body of material was gigantic, and I realized that I would have to limit it. The first step was a natural one, through the premise that all the patterns I adapted must be able to be knitted by others — not just by expert knitters, but knitters of average skills should be able to knit most of them. As a further limitation, I chose to work only with 2-stitch wide strips, so that no more than four stitches ever crossed.

Many of the interlaced patterns shown in this book are also found in the Celtic ornamental idiom, as these two peoples had considerable contact through the years. I have, however, found the patterns in Scandinavian artifacts. The Vikings were cosmopolitan and often took inspiration from other cultures, but never copied directly. They always integrated the new elements into their own language of form and design.

In the same way, I have tried to manage a cultural heritage by translating old patterns to the newer technique of knitting—the Vikings would certainly have done it themselves if they had knitted—and to make them live again by integrating them into my own language of form, by creating modern, wearable clothing.

I hardly suspected when I set out that the handcraft of the Vikings would occupy so much of my life, but after five years of intensive work, Viking patterns are truly interwoven into my design. This includes a traveling exhibition, *Knitting on the Trail of the Vikings*, and a systematic account in book form—the one you are now reading. Sometimes, that's how it goes!

Bird figure from Gårdby, Öland, Sweden

Analyzing Viking Patterns

There's no shortage of descriptions of Viking ornamentation. Innumerable theses have been written on styles, dating, rune inscribers, and so forth, but I know of no other that has had the pattern—the braiding technique—itself as the starting point, and then traced it back on different artifacts to various places.

Pattern analysis can be done at different levels. The most superficial, which is also the clearest, is the pattern unit, or repeat.

At that level, the pattern can be altered by such relational changes as staggering the repeats in relation to one another, flipping it mirror image horizontally or vertically, or coupling it with other pattern repeats.

The deepest level comprises different technical manipulations—whether to use knit or purl stitches, increases and decreases, cable crosses and such. At this level is found the technical innovation which made possible rendering the Viking interlaced patterns shown here as knitting and which has two components.

One is the twisted increase which makes possible increasing in two adjacent stitches without disturbing the structure of the fabric or making a hole. The other is the siting of the increases and decreases.

If there is an increase every round or every second round, should the first decrease lie on the next purl row, directly after the last traveling stitch or on the next knit row after that? After having systematically tried a number of different solutions, I decided on this (below), as it is the easiest to knit and works well in most cases. How to knit these units is described in detail under "The New Technique" in the back of the book.

Paired increases

Paired deceases

In a few of the designs (Lillbjärs) I have placed the increase a row later and the decreases a row earlier. That means that the increases are done from the purl side and the decreases are purl stitches, which makes the pattern a little harder to knit.

On a level in between, one works with a visual element smaller than the entire pattern but comprising many technical manipulations: the pattern can be vertical bands or diagonals, or a motif like the *single-strand mat knot* or the *S-curve*.

Other elements are the whole group of paired increases with the first traveling stitches that follow them, here called "the start," or the last traveling stitches of an element with the paired decreases which follow them, here called "the finish."

These "starts" and "finishes" are units that appear again and again in different contexts.

There is a centered start with a corresponding finish, a twisted start,

Stone cross from Brompton, Yorkshire, England.
Included in the ornamentation are narrow and wide mat knots.

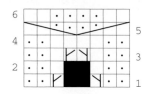

Centered start

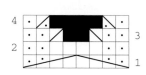

Centered finish

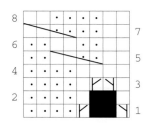

Right directional start

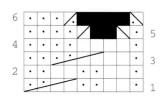

Right directional finish

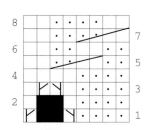

Left directional start

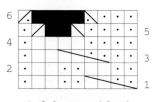

Left directional finish

which can be twisted either left or right, each with its corresponding finish.

Notice that the placement of the increases and decreases are all identical: what makes them different is the first traveling stitches.

My experimental work shifted continually between these three levels, but most of the work lay on the middle level. Here, lines and motifs of the pattern are the focus, and one must learn the "grammar" of the pattern type.

In cabled patterns, one can work with diagonal and vertical lines. Horizontals are not natural for the pattern type and need special solutions.

One must not forget that the increases take up four, and the decreases two, rows of vertical space, which calls for a certain vertical distance between pattern repeats. As virtually all the pattern formation happens on the knit side, one needn't really think about the purl rows—except to remember that the last decrease is on the purl side.

I start a job most often with a pencil sketch. If it's an analysis of a pattern from a Viking artifact, I look at the artifact and try to break down the pattern into vertical and diagonal lines, right and left crosses, etc.

When I am looking for variations or creating my own patterns, I often start with a motif and might try flipping it mirror image, and work after that with different placements and different ways to knit up the pattern. Other times, I begin with a band of pattern and try to see what happens when I change a couple of strands—for example, a narrow band with small latticework or a wide band with small latticework.

The next step is, with the pencil sketch as a basis, to try to chart the pattern. Afterward, I might try to knit it to be sure that the pattern functions and that the knitted pattern looks as expected. The first try

often leads to small adjustments and re-knitting.

The process from artifact to sweater is thus very protracted, and not unusually side trails that appear are the most exciting to follow. The results of such work, in a systematized form, are shown in the next part of this book.

Sketch and artifact: Carving of Sigurd Fafnersbane fighting the dragon on a stone from York, England.

Rings and Chains

One of the simplest and most basic motifs in all ornamentation is the ring. During the Iron Age, it was often used in the form of a circle with a dot in the middle, to decorate simple articles like spoons and combs. Ornamentation is usually more complicated, but many shapes can be read as rings twisted in various ways to give them a different appearance.

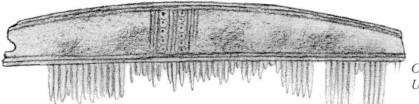

Comb from Birka, Uppland, Sweden

The first two patterns are a small and a larger ring. The small ring consists of a start and a finish. The larger ring is created by having the strands travel two stitches to each side. The ring can be endlessly enlarged by further outward traveling stitches.

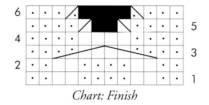

Chart: Finish

Chart: Start

Adding a cable cross between the beginning and the end makes an eight or a standing infinity sign. On a reliquary cross from Tønsberg, Norway, which dates to about 1000 A.D., this sign is repeated as a frame for a cross. The motif can also be considered a ring twisted once in the middle.

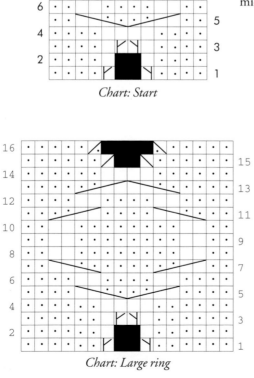

Chart: Large ring

Reliquary cross from Tønsberg, Norway

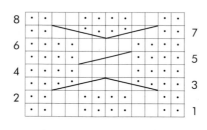

Chart: A crossing to be inserted between a start and a finish.

Left: Pattern swatch, standing infinity sign.

Right: Sword from Valsgärde, Uppland, Sweden.

Bottom: Picture stone from Smiss, Gotland, Sweden.

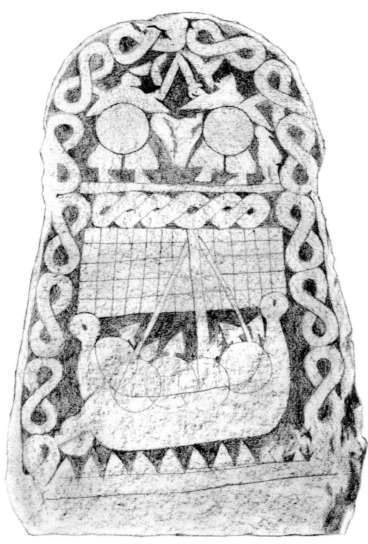

A repetition of this unit results in an open cable, appearing like two ropes that twine around each other, or, with closed ends, like a twisted ring. A closed cabling like this was used to decorate a sword from a 7th century grave in Valsgärde, Uppland, while an unbroken cabling edges a shield boss, also from Valsgärde. Both the closed cable and the standing infinity sign can be seen on a picture stone from Smiss, Gotland (Sweden). We can only guess what symbolic meaning it may have had at the time.

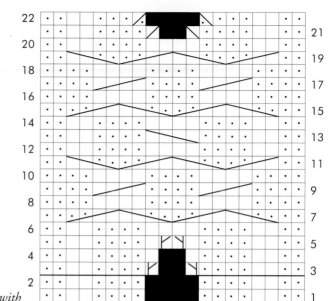

Chart: Panel with quartered, interlaced ring

In the following pattern (above), the large ring has been woven around the intersection of two ropes. Our first sweater, *Hermod,* has the same ring, with a sparse lattice of rope woven through it.

Beyond these two patterns, all the designs in this chapter can be seen as rings, which in different ways are twisted or linked up to form long or short chains. The distance between the motifs in all of these chains can be altered by knitting the straight portion (Rows 1 and 2 on the chart) the desired number of rounds.

Left: Pattern swatch: narrow closed cable.

Center: the artifact the pattern was taken from, a shield buckler (?) from Valsgärde, Uppland, Sweden.

Quartered or interlaced ring, shown above as a pattern swatch and below in a magnified detail from the Skabersjö buckle, Skåne, Sweden.

HERMOD
Twisted linked rings in a pullover with detached hood

The shape and materials of this sweater were inspired by the cassocks of medieval monks. The pattern is a variant of Ring with interlaced ropes, but here junctions of a open latticework are woven through the rings. The detached hood (which can of course be sewn on if you wish) give the sweater drama. Without the hood, it has a more everyday tone. The yarn, a recycled product of mainly wool and cotton, has a little stiffness—crispness—to it.

Size: One size

Measurements of finished garment: bust, 48¾ in/124 cm. Length, 27½ in/70 cm.

Materials: 18 balls of Cotton Lambswool Evergreen Collection for sweater. 5 balls for the hood. 1 button each for sweater and hood.

Equipment: 5 mm and 5.5 mm knitting needles.

Tension: 16 sts and 23 rows in stockinette on 5.5 mm knitting needles = 4 inches square or 10 x 10 cm. Check tension before you start project.

Note: The reason that the number of sts at the top of the neck are different in front and in back, and that the number of sts in the neck opening plus the shoulders are more than the number of sts cast on, is because pattern increases are included in the count.

Back

On 5 mm needles, cast on 98 stitches. Knit 7 rows (garter stitch). Change to 5.5 mm needles and knit following chart for 3 repeats plus 30 rows (about 26¾ in/68 cm). Put the center 30 sts on a string and knit each side separately. Bind off shoulder in 3 steps at beginning of every 2nd row, beginning at outside edge: 11, 16, 13 sts. Break yarn and pull through last stitch. Reverse this for the opposite shoulder.

Front

Knit like the back for 3 repeats of the chart plus 16 rows (about 24½ in/62 cm). Place the center 16 sts on a string and knit each side separately. On the neck edge, dec 1 st every second row 8 times. Bind off for the shoulders at the same height (26¾ in/68 cm) and in the same way as on the back.

Sleeves

With 5 mm needles, cast on 40 sts and knit 7 rows [garter st]. Change to 5.5 mm needles and knit the pattern following the chart, increasing 1 st at both edges every 4th row 18 times (= 76 sts) (Include) the new sts in the pattern after they are added). When the sleeve measures about 17 in/43 cm, bind off. Knit yet another, identical to the first.

Assembling

Block the pieces separately. Sew the right shoulder together. *Neck edge*: With 5 mm needles, pick up 76 sts around the neck, starting at the left shoulder. Knit (back and forth) 6 rows and bind off on the 7th. Sew the left shoulder together up to the garter stitches. Crochet a little loop on the front edge of the garter stitches and sew a button on the back edge. *Sleeves and side seams:* Sew the sleeves to the body, matching the center of the sleeve top with the shoulder seam. Allow about 9¾ in/25 cm for the armhole, front and back. Sew the underarm and side seam in continuously.

Hood

On 5 mm needles, cast on 106 sts and k 6 rows back and forth. K the pattern and short rows (See "Short Rows" in back of book) beginning on a purl row as follows: Beginning at point A in the chart, purl (or k according to the chart) 11 sts (not counting increase for the pattern), turn, yarn over, and knit back. Knit 4 sts beyond the turning point, knitting the yarn over with the st following it, turn, yarn over, and knit back. Do this a total of 4 times (2 are already completed.), knitting 4 sts beyond the turning point each time. Knit to the opposite edge of work and k short rows the opposite direction, starting at point B on the chart. Then k even until work measures about 9¾ in/25 cm at center back. Mark center st and dec on both sides of it 1 st every row 3 times and 2 sts every second row 3 times. Distribute the sts on 2 needles with the points toward the front edge, and with knit sides facing, k together while binding off (See directions for knitted bind off in back of book.)

With 5 mm needle, pick up about 100 sts around the front edge of the hood and k 6 rows (garter st). Bind off on the wrong side. Sew a loop on the right front edge and a button on the left.

In *Linked Rings* two large rings have been linked to each other and create a motif. The source is the decoration of a shield plate from Vendel in Uppland, Sweden, where the rings form a chain. A number of experiments showed

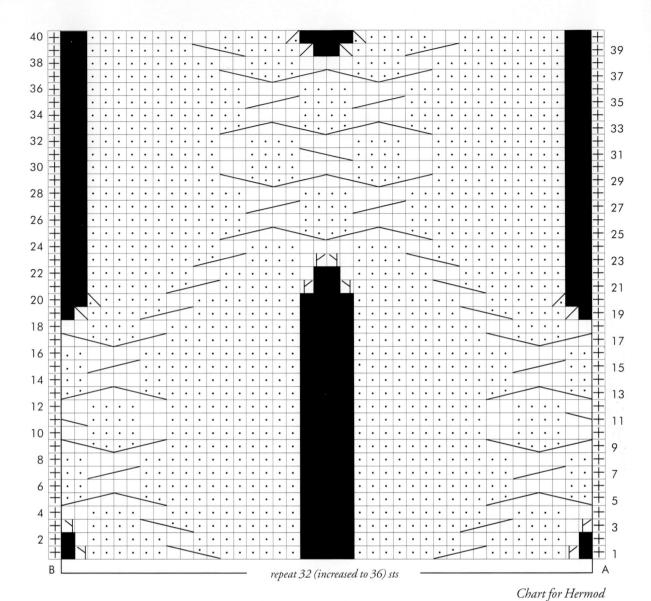

B   repeat 32 (increased to 36) sts   A

Chart for Hermod

Hermod: detail of neckband

that it was not possible to knit such a running chain and maintain the character of the links. Each link in the chain became either too long and narrow or became too thin for its size.

Pattern swatch for Linked rings

In the following two patterns, the ends of large rings have been twisted to form loops. These loops can then be linked together with spaces in between. The open variant shown here as a sketch, a pattern swatch, and a chart, is used in *Siv*, the pullover on the following page. A denser, interwoven braiding of two ring ends is shown after the directions.

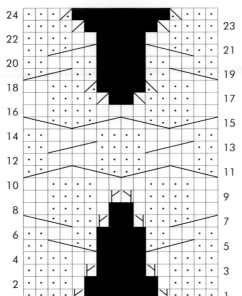

Chart: Linked rings

Twisted linked rings, as a pattern swatch above and a chart below.

Shield plate from Vendel, Uppland [Sweden].

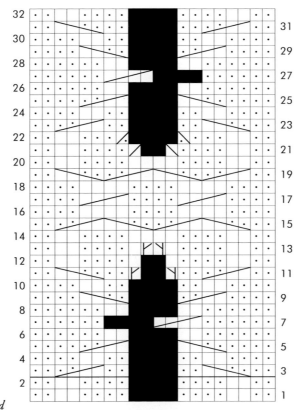

Chart: Twisted linked rings

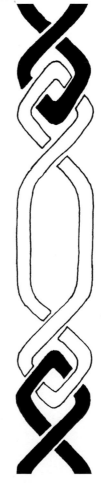

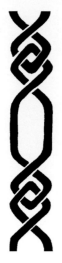

Siv
Classic pullover with chain links and ribbing

Siv is a classic shape with inset sleeves. The long, linked, twisted rings lined with narrow ribbing have a powerful graphic effect on the wide bands of plain stockinette. The length of the sweater is determined by the number of rows in the repeat. You can change the sweater's length by lengthening or shortening the "straightaway" distances.

Finished measurements: Bust, 34½/88 (37¾/96) 40/102 (42½108) in/cm. Length: 24¾ in/63 cm.

Materials: 7 (7) 8 (9) 50 gram skeins Silketweed (or Soft Woolsilk).

Needles: 2.5 mm and 3 mm needles.

Tension: 25 sts x 34 rows in stockinette on 3 mm needles = 4 inches square or 10 x 10 cm. The 24 sts of the pattern band (16 sts + the ribs on both sides) x 50 rows = 3 x 6 inches/7.5 x 15 cm. Check your tension carefully while knitting.

Pattern: Follow chart for *Cable with linked rings* on p. 19. Rows 1 and 2 are repeated 10 times between motifs, the height of 1 repeat is 50 rows.

Back

With 2.5 mm needles, cast on 122 (130) 138 (146) sts and rib: k 2, p 2, for 1¼ in/3 cm. The 2 outermost sts on each side should be knitted on the right side of work. Change to 3 mm needles and, not counting the 2 k sts on each edge, k 14 (18) 22 (26) sts in stockinette, *(p 2, k 2) twice, p 2, inc 1 p st, p 2, inc 1 p st, p 2 (= 8 consecutive purl sts), (k 2, p 2) twice, k 14 stockinette. Repeat from * 3 times and end with k 0 (4) 8 (12) sts = 128 (136) 144 (152) sts. In following rows, keep all purl sts purl, all knit sts knit. The center panel begins by repeating Rows 1 and 2 ten times. The pattern bands on the sides begin with Row 3 in chart. When work measures 16½/42 (16/41) 16/41 (15¾/40) in/cm, bind off for armhole: Bind off 3 (4) 5 (6) sts every row and each edge twice, then dec 1 st each edge every other row 5 (6) 7 (8) times = 106 (108) 110 (112) sts. K even. When armhole measures 8½/21 (8¾/22) 8¾/22 (9/23) in/cm, put center 50 (50) 52 (52) sts on a holder and k each side separately. Bind off on shoulder sides 9, 9, 10 (9, 10, 10) 9, 10, 10 (10, 10, 10) sts.

Front

K front like back until armhole measures 5/13 (5¼/14) 5½/14 (6/15) in/cm. Put center 26 (26) 28 (28) sts on a holder for neck and knit each side separately. Bind off on neck side, 2 sts 3 times and then dec 1 st every other row 6 times. Bind off shoulder at the same height and in the same way as on back. Repeat, mirror image, on the other side of neckline and opposite shoulder.

Sleeves

With 2.5 mm needles, cast on 50 (50) 54 (54) sts and rib, k 2, p 2, for 1¼ in/3 cm, making sure you have k 2 (k 2) p 2 (p 2) on outside edges of right side of work. Change to 3 mm needles and k 14 (14) 16 (16), (p 2, k 2) twice, p 3, inc 1 p, p 2, inc 1 p, p 3 (= 10 p sts), (k 2, p 2) twice, k 14 (14) 16 (16) = 52 (52) 56 (56) sts. In following rows, keep all p sts purl and all k sts, knit. The pattern panel begins by repeating Rows 1 and 2 ten times.

Inc 1 st each side every 6th row 17 (20) 21 (24) times = 86 (92) 98 (104) sts. When sleeve measures about 17 in/43 cm, bind off for underarm 3 (4) 5 (6) sts each side and then dec 1 st each side every other row until 34 sts remain. Bind off 2 sts at beginning of every row 4 times. Bind off. Knit another, identical, sleeve.

Assembly

Block all pieces. Sew right shoulder seam. *Neckline:* On 2.5 mm needles, pick up 112 (112) 116 (116) sts around neck and rib for 1¼ in/3 cm (Dec where needed so that the pattern ribs continue into ribbing). Bind off in ribbing. Sew left shoulder and left neckline. Sew sleeves into arm holes, centering sleeve at shoulder seam, then sew sleeve and side seams continuously.

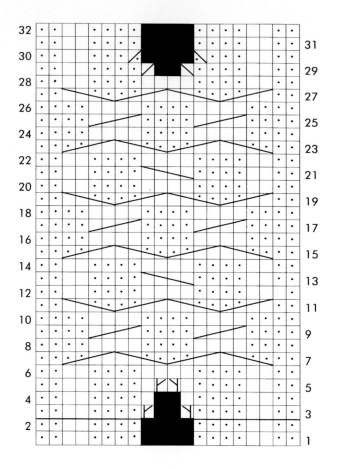

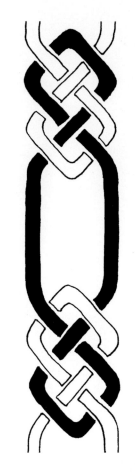

The denser variant of linked rings, *interlaced twisted rings,* was found on a harness plate in Stavanger, Norway, and on a bone fragment from York, England, and other places.

Think of the difference between this and the preceding pattern as the difference between shaking hands with someone and taking that person by the underarm from the same angle.

Knitted pattern swatch, chart and sketch for Interlaced Twisted Rings.

The illustrations show a ornamental harness plate from Stavanger, Norway, and a bone fragment from York, England.

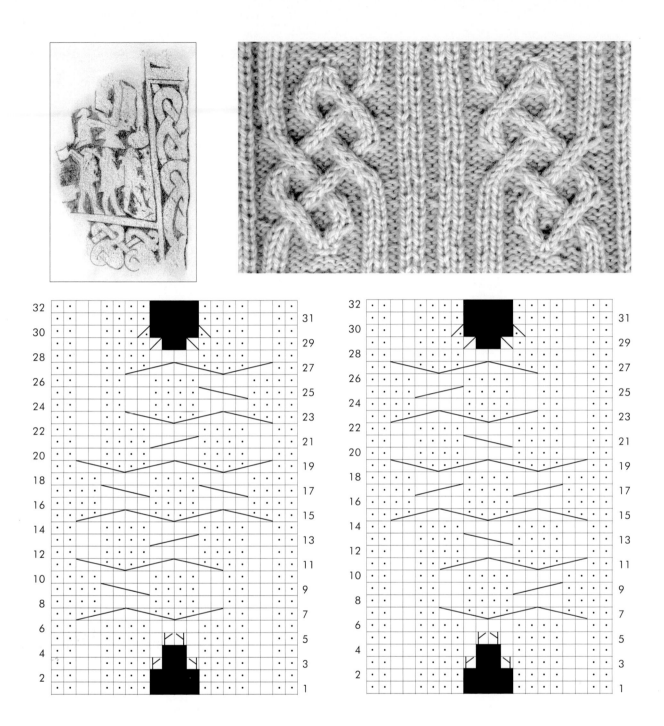

Upper left: Detail from bas relief at Alskogs Kyrka, Gotland, Sweden.

The pattern swatch, upper right, shows Bjärs Hitches with its matching mirror image.

I called this *Bjärs Hitches* because the first example of it I found was on a sword sheath from Bjärs, Gotland (Sweden). In any case, it's not a common motif. One of the few other examples I discovered was on the edge of a picture stone from Alskogs Church on Gotland.

The basic element is the same as in the linked and the interlaced rings above—a ring which is twisted to create an eye at each end. Here the eyes have been set on the diagonal and linked asymetrically, creating the appearance of interlaced half-hitches. This is shown most clearly in the sketch on p. 26.

Fjörgyn
Jacket and hood covered with ropey half-hitches

The color speaks of stone and the shape of a soft woolly Icelandic sheep. Opposites meet in this sweater which is almost a cape — large and scrumptious with a generous hood and big pockets. Add a windproof lining and you'll have great outerwear for fall and early spring.

Sizes: One size will fit small, medium, and large
Finished measurements: Bust, 51 in/130 cm. Length, 33in/84 cm.
Materials: 16 balls Lopi. 7 buttons
Needles: 5.5 and 6 mm needles
Tension: 13 sts and 18 rows in stockinette on 6 mm needles = 4 inches square or 10 x 10 cm. Knit a tension swatch and change your needle size if necessary.
Please note: The front has no neckline and the pattern on the front continues without interruption onto the hood.

Left front

With 5.5 mm needles, cast on 63 sts and rib, p 2, k 2, for 3¼ in/8 cm, making sure there are 2 k sts on the knit side at both ends inside the selvage sts. Start pattern, following chart a-e and a-b and maintaining knit selvage sts, starting at Rows 0 + 00 (**Note** the decreases in Row 0, which line up ribs in pattern with ribbed edge.) and then Rows 1-32. Continue to knit pattern a-b on the 21 sts of front pattern panel, but k remaining sts as *pocket edging*: Knit ribbing, k 2, p 2, and *inc* in pattern so that pattern ribs continue into ribbing. When ribbing is 1½ in/4 cm long, bind off pocket sts in ribbing, letting the 21 sts from front pattern panel rest while you knit *inside of the pocket*: With 6 mm needles, cast on 30 sts and knit stockinette for 30 rows. Place this piece next to front edge panel and join them. Continue knitting on 6 mm needles in stockinette on stitches continuing up from pocket and continue pattern on front edge panel. When work measures about 30 in/76 cm, bind off on sleeve side for shoulder: bind off 5 sts 6 times (at the beginning of every second row). Place remaining 21 sts of front border on a holder.

Right front

Knit mirror image to the left front, following the chart c-e for front panel and a-d for pocket.

Back

On 5.5 mm needles, cast on 86 sts and rib k 2, p 2 for 8 cm, taking care to start and end with 2 k sts on right side of work. Change to 6 mm needles and stockinette st. Knit even until work measures 30 in/76 cm. Bind off shoulders, 5 sts 6 times each side and put remaining 26 sts on a holder.

Sleeves

With 5.5 mm needles, cast on 82 sts and rib, p 2, k 2, for 3 in/8 cm. Then start pattern: k a-e and a-d starting with chart Row 0 and Row 00. Dec as shown in Row 0 (to continue ribs into pattern) = 74 sts, then change to 6 mm needles and knit Rows 1-32 on chart. When pattern ends, k stockinette, inc 1 st each side every 10th row 3 times = 80 sts. When stockinette measures about 7 in/18 cm, bind off 5 sts at beginning of each row until 20 sts remain. Bind off. Knit another, identical sleeve.

Assembly

Block all pieces. Sew shoulder seams. *Hood*: On 6 mm needles, pick up the sts on holders = 68 sts. Place a marker on both sides of the 26 sts continued from the back and inc 1 st before and after the marker, using right and left leaning incs as shown in chart. Inc both sides of markers every second row 5 times = 88 sts. When hood measures about 11 in/28 cm, place a marker at center back and k 2 together before and SSK after marker every second row 3 times and then k 3 together and double SSK every second row 3 times. Bind off and sew top together. *Left front edge*: On 5.5 mm needles, pick up 147 sts along left front edge and hood and rib, k 2, p 2, for 1½ in/4 cm. Be sure to start and end with 2 k sts on right side of work. Bind off in ribbing. Mark positions of buttons: Place the lowest in the middle of the lower edge ribbing, the highest about at the middle of the 4th pattern repeat. Space the remaining five evenly between them. *Right front edge*: Follow directions for left front edge, but place buttonholes opposite the button markers. Begin k 2, p 2 ribbing but after ½ inch/ 1.5 cm, knit buttonhole across 3 sts, opposite markers on the left front edge. Graft the little ribbed edges at top of hood together (See "Tips and Tricks.") Sew sleeves onto body, centering sleeve top on shoulder seam, and allowing 11¾ in/30 cm front and back for armhole. Sew underarm and side seam continuously. Sew sides and tack down bottom of pockets, invisibly, on the inside. Sew on buttons.

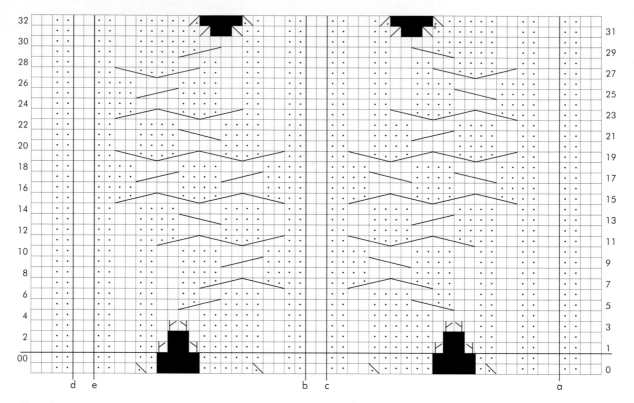

Chart for Fjörgyn

The pattern swatch below shows the angular Bjärs Hitches pattern. The diagram at right shows clearly the difference between the angular and the rounded variants.

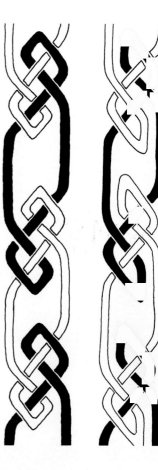

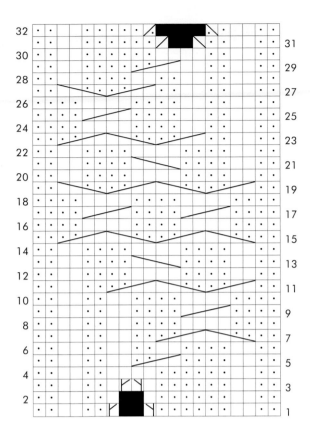

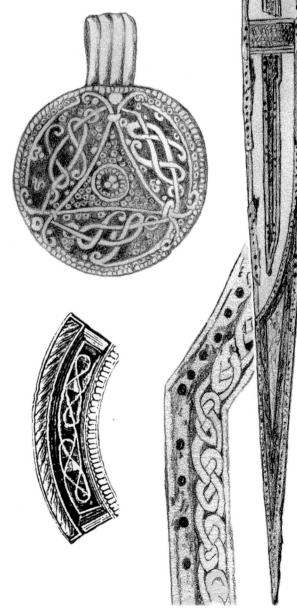

Charts: Mirror-image variants of the angular Bjärs Hitches.

Right: Sword sheath from Hejnum, Bjärs, Gotland (Sweden) with an enlarged detail of the decorative metalwork.

Below: Pendant from Honskatten, Norway, detail.

Detail of bronze strap ornament found in Trondheim, Norway.

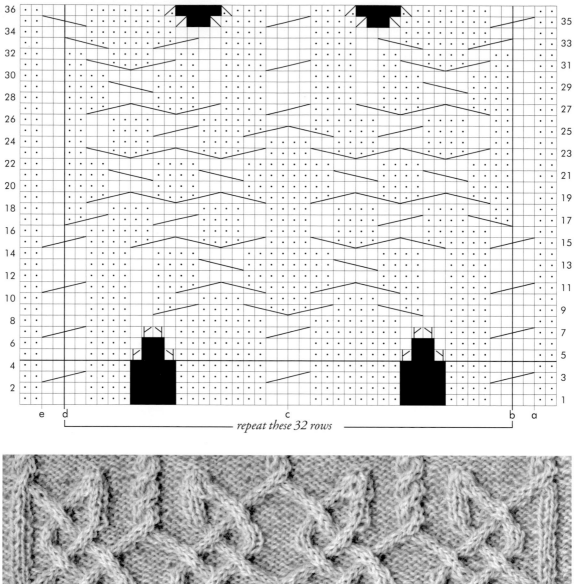

36 · · | · · · · · | · · 35
34 · · · · · · · · · · · · 33
32 · · · · · · · · · · · 31
30 · · · · · · · · · · · · 29
28 · · · · · · · · · · · · 27
26 · · · · · · · · · · · · 25
24 · · · · · · · · · · · · 23
22 · · · · · · · · · · · · 21
20 · · · · · · · · · · · · 19
18 · · · · · · · · · · · · 17
16 · · · · · · · · · · · · 15
14 · · · · · · · · · · · · 13
12 · · · · · · · · · · · · 11
10 · · · · · · · · · · · · 9
8 · · · · · · · · · · · · 7
6 · · · · · · · · · · · · 5
4 · · · · · · · · · · · · 3
2 · · · · · · · · · · · · 1

e   d   c   b   a

repeat these 32 rows

28

In the next pattern, I combined the angular left and right Bjärs hitch pattern with cables to produce an allover pattern. This can of course also be applied to the more rounded version, as shown below.

If only one horizontal repeat is knitted, with the two outermost ropes knitted straight (there is no room for cabling), the result is a smart, broad vertical panel. If instead one knits from c on the chart to d, then from b to c, the repeat is centered differently, the corners of the half hitches point in the opposite direction, resulting in a similar panel with an entirely different look. Yet another variant would result if one knitted from a-e, so that the cable was included on the sides.

Chart and pattern swatch opposite show the angular Bjärs hitches as an allover pattern.

At lower right, the more rounded version as an allover pattern.

Above that, the elements from the allover pattern are paraphrased two different ways for vertical bands of pattern. If you wish to knit this, compose your own chart on grid paper first.

Happiness sign, or
St. John's Cross

This happiness sign, or St. John's cross, was common in the Viking representational idiom, and is found in different versions on all kinds of things. It was thought to bring happiness and often appears on jewelry, for example on the little pendant from Gråträsk, Piteå, (Sweden), or the tiny knob of a fibula from Eketorp, Närke, (Sweden).

It too can be seen as open loops of a ring. Most commonly, the ring has only three loops, but four also appear regularly.

Knit-technically, it's difficult to get a handsome shape for the three-looped happiness sign, but the one with four loops is presented here in two sizes.

A happiness sign on a sword hilt from Hedeby, Denmark, shows a ring threaded through the four loops, a design also found on a striking gold buckle from Hornelund, Denmark. On this buckle one can also see an example of the 3-bight happiness sign.

In the last happiness sign pattern, I've taken off one loop so that the knot can be attached to a cable. The same "broken" knot forms the breaking crest of waves on a picture stone from Lillbjärs, (Sweden). The pattern is offered on a following page in two mirror image versions.

Top: a little pendant from Gråträsk, Norrbotten (Sweden).

Left and below: Chart and pattern swatch for the smaller happiness sign (St. John's Cross).

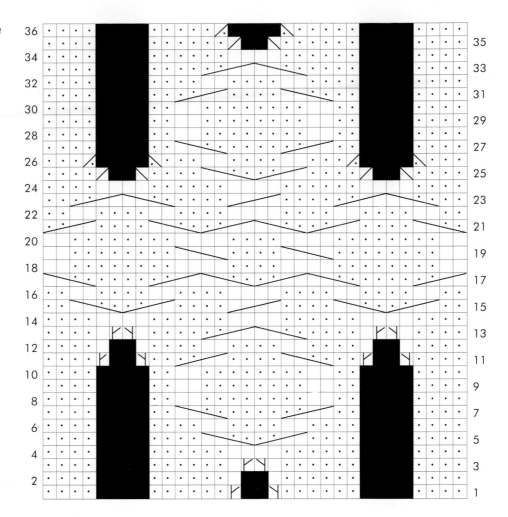

Top: Chart and pattern swatch for the larger happiness sign. This was used as a motif on Frode, *for which you can find directions in "Plaited Mats."*

Far lower right, the little end-knob of a fibula from Eketorpsskatten (Sweden).

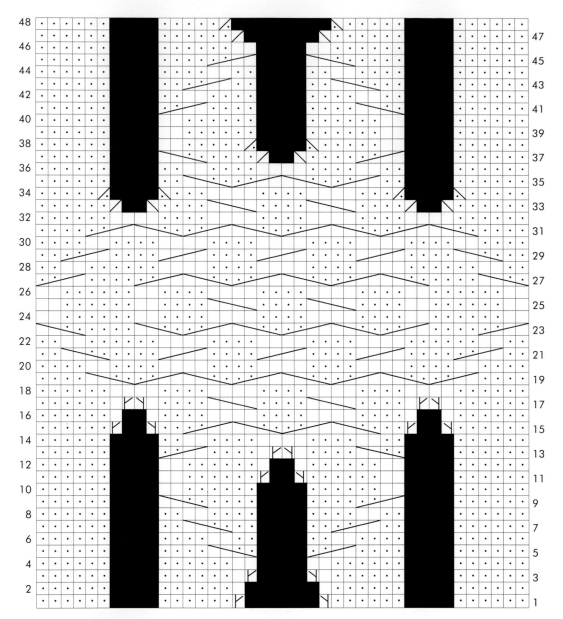

Chart: Happiness sign woven through a ring.

Illustrations: Far left: Sword hilt from Hedeby (originally Denmark but now part of Germany) showing the happiness sign quartering a ring.

Left: Detail from picture stone from Lillbjärs with a three-bight happiness sign used to represent the breaking crest of a wave. Perhaps a way of hobbling the ocean's power?

Pattern swatch showing happiness sign woven through a ring (left) and opposite three-bight happiness signs on cables (right)

Illustrations: A buckle from Hornelund, Denmark.

Chart: Opposite facing, three-bight happiness signs on cables, as shown in pattern swatch above.

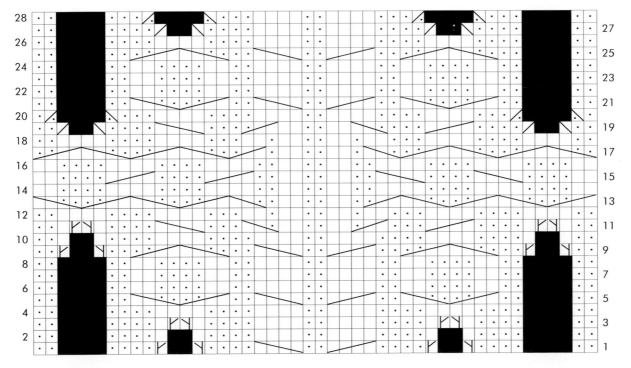

Horizontal Zigzags

Zigzag ornamentation is widespread through many cultures and periods. It was common during the iron age and for a long time thereafter.

On the more splendid objects, the craftsman wasn't satisfied with an simple zigzag but decorated each point with a little loop.

A strip of such "curlicues" decorates a shield plate from Valsgärde (Sweden). On another plate on the same shield, a knotted braid ends in a couple of curlicues. The motif appears again on the magnificent metal plate from the Brahe Church door in Visingsö (Sweden), and on the edge of a clasp from Skabersjö, two such curly zigzags are laid together to form a double one.

This chapter offers no directions for a whole garment with horizontal bands of pattern, but with the diagram and the pattern swatches, you can insert them into any garment you feel is suited to widthwise ornamentation.

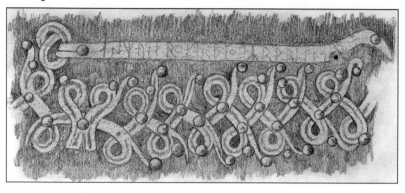

Above: Plate from Brahekyrkans (church) door, Visingsö, Småland, southern Sweden.

Below left: Detail of zigzag border on a belt buckle from Sösdala, Skåne, southern Sweden.

Facing page:

Bottom: Chart and pattern swatch for two zigzag variants.

Illustrations:

Plate from Ultuna, Uppland, Sweden (the little snake).

Enlarged detail of buckle from Skabersjö, Skåne, Sweden.

Far right: Buckler from Valsgärde, Uppland, Sweden.

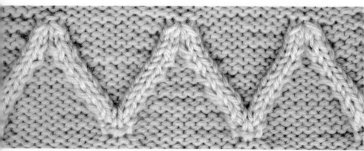

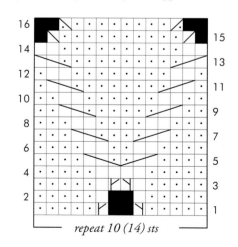

repeat 10 (14) sts

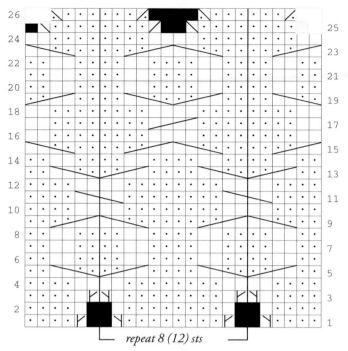

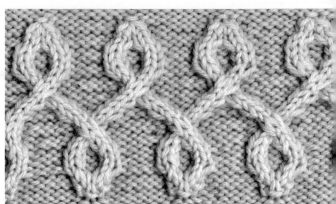

repeat 8 (12) sts

repeat 8 (12) sts

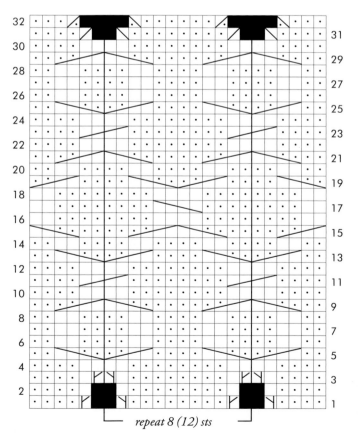

Plaited mats

Plaiting, or braiding, was clearly the dominant artistic theme in the Viking era. Often the braid had a distinctly animal character and was freely interwoven, but more formal plaitwork without a mammalian stamp was also common.

This chapter takes up a number of pattern variations. Four sweaters and two caps provide examples of ways plaited mats can be used on knitted garments.

In the Viking artistic idiom, animals, dragons, serpents, deer, and other beings, in more or less stylized forms, twined around one another rather freely. Here and there, animals are easily identifiable: you see a head, legs, or feet or, often, a haunch indicated with a circle or a spiral, but other times the animal elements are stylized almost beyond recognition. The bodies become drawn out strands and it is often only the width of the strand that indicates it represents a serpent or a dragon.

Viking fascination with plaiting was also expressed in stylized, graphically simple patterns consisting of a number of strands systematically plaited over and under one another. This sort of braided pattern is what we will look at more closely here.

The simplest plait is a cable of two twined strands. This cable was shown in the first chapter, where the strands create a twisted ring by connecting the ends at the start and finish of the plait.

Three strips make an asymmetric braid, the classic hair braid or pigtail. Plaits braided from an uneven number of strands can't be closed, as closure requires an even number of strips.

Plaited mats with four and six strands are described in detail below, followed by free variations.

Narrow mats

The narrow mat of four interwoven strands is a common border on Viking artifacts, including the buckle from Skabersjö above.

The detail is enlarged, and the entire buckle, a tiny pattern sampler in itself, is shown elsewhere in the book.

On the tombstone from Hellvi, Gotland (Sweden), the plaits are closed in order to fill out the margins on both sides of the central picture. This is discussed in more detail in the section on narrow braided motifs that follows.

Top: Detail from Skabersjö buckle, Skåne, Sweden.

Left: Tombstone from Hellvi, Gotland, Sweden.

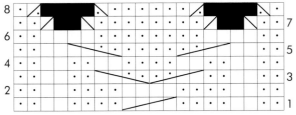

Centered finish

Centered finish

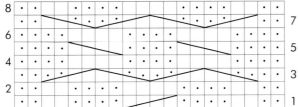

Directional finish

Lattice repeat

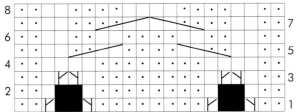

Directional start

Centered start

Pattern swatch: Narrow lattice mat with angular start and finish.

37

HERVOR
Pullover and cap

Interwoven mats of various kinds were frequently used by the Viking artisans as space fillers, ending when they reached a corner or the edge of a limited surface, as on the tombstone from Hellvi, Gotland on the previous page. Here I have chosen to use the decorative effect of unbounded closures within the area and have added a motif of linked rings.

Sizes: S (M) L (XL)

Finished measurements: Bust, 39½/100 (42½/108) 45½/116 (48¾/124) in/cm. Length, 20¾/53 (21¾/55) 22½/57 (23¼/59) in/cm. Head measurement: 21½-22½ in/55-57 cm.

Materials: 8 (9) 10 (12) skeins Rowan DK Tweed + 2 skeins for the cap.

Needles: 3 mm and 4 mm needles. Circular needles sizes 3 and 4 mm, 40 cm long.

Tension: 20 sts in stockinette on 4 mm needles = 4 in/10 cm. Make a test swatch, and adjust your needle size up for too many, down for too few sts per 4 in/10 cm. Check your tension now and then while knitting.

Pattern: Knitted from *Narrow lattice (pattern repeat), Directional Start* and *Directional Finish (p. 37)* and *Chart for Linked Rings,* below.

Back

On 3 mm needles cast on 102 (110) 118 (126) stitches and set up patterns, starting on the wrong side of work: A: p 2, k 2 for 18 (22) 26 (30) sts, ending with p 2. Place marker. B: k 2 sts, p 2, k 4, p 4, k 4, p 2, k 2. (This is Row 8 of *narrow lattice (pattern repeat)* on p. 37 and sets up the sts for Row 1, the first k row.) Place marker. C: p 2, k 2, for 26 sts ending with p 2. Place marker. D: Same as B. Place marker. E: Same as A. Turn and k the right side, ribbing k into k, p into p, and inserting row 1 of *Narrow lattice (pattern repeat)* in B and D. When work measures 4 in/10 cm, change to 4 mm needles and knit reverse stockinette above the ribbing (purl side facing out). At 7/18 (7½/19) 8/20 (8½/21) in/cm, begin the linked ring motif on the center 2 sts, following *Linked rings* chart (this page). Immediately above this and also centered on the center two sts, begin another panel of lattice, starting this time with *Directional start* (p. 37, 4th chart from top) and continuing with *Narrow lattice (pattern repeat)* just above it on p. 37. At 12½/32 (13/33) 13½/34 (14/35) in/cm,

dec for armhole both sides 1 st every other row 5 (6) 7 (8) times = 92 (98) 104 (110) sts. At the same time, finish the 2 outside panels following *Directional finish* chart on p. 37, and directly above that, k a *linked rings* motif, following the chart on this page. When armhole measures 8¼/21 (8¾/22) 9/23 (9½/24) in/cm, put the center 38 sts on a holder and bind off shoulders.

Front

Knit front like the back until work measures about 19/48 (19½/50) 20½/52 (21¼/54) in/cm. Place the center 22 sts on a holder and k each shoulder separately: Both shoulders: Dec on neck side 2 sts every other row twice, then 1 st every other row 4 times. Bind off shoulders when both front and back are the same length.

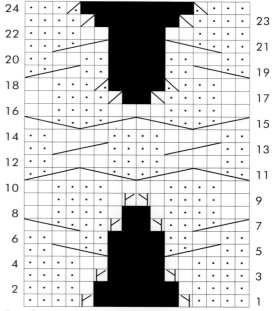

Chart for Linked rings motif. Other charts for this design are on the preceding page.

Sleeves

With 3 mm needles, cast on 48 (48) 56 (56) sts and set up patterns (working from the wrong side in the first row): A: Rib, p 2, k 2, for 14 (14) 18 (18) sts, ending with p 2. Place marker. B: K 2 sts, p 2, k 4, p 4, k 4, p 2, k 2 (This is Row 8 of *Narrow lattice (pattern repeat)* on p. 37, a wrong side row, and sets up the sts for Row 1, the first k row = 20 sts). Place marker. C: Repeat A. Turn and begin right side of sleeve, ribbing in A, then in B start at Row 1, *Narrow lattice (pattern repeat)* on p. 37. Rib in C. Continue in pattern for 4 in/10 cm.

Change to 4 mm needles and begin knitting reverse stockinette above the ribbing (purl side facing out). Inc 1 st both sides every 4th row altogether 18 (19) 17 (18) times = 84 (86) 90 (92) sts. When work measures 13 in/33 cm, *finish* the pattern using the chart for *Directional finish* on p. 37. Directly above this, knit *Linked rings* (Chart on lower right, p. 38). When sleeve measures 18 in/46 cm, dec for sleeve cap: Dec 1 st each side of every second row 5 (6) 7 (8) times. Bind off.

Assembly

Block all pieces to measure between damp towels and let them dry completely. Sew shoulder seams. *Neckband*: With 3 mm circular needle, pick up 98 sts around the neck and continue pattern panels up middle front and back, with k 2 p 2 ribbing on the remaining sts. When neckband measures 3 in/8 cm, bind off in ribbing. Sew sleeves on, placing center sts at shoulder seam.

Sew underarm and side seams continuously.

Cap

On 4 mm needles, cast on 18 sts and knit the center 18 sts of *Narrow lattice (pattern repeat)* on p. 37, starting with Row 8 on the wrong side. When work measures about 19½ in/50 cm and you reach Row 1, graft ends together, mimicking k and p sts, and crossing the 4 center sts, 2 over 2 to right. Pull seam so it doesn't bulge. *Crown*: with circular needle, pick up 96 sts along one side of band, k 2 in every st around = 192 sts. K reverse stockinette for 3 in/8 cm. On next rnd, k 2 sts together around = 96 sts. Divide these 96 sts in 8 groups of 12 sts. Dec: at the beginning and end of each group, p 2 sts together every 5th rnd until 16 sts remain. K 2 together all the way around, then break yarn, thread tail through remaining sts, and pull up firmly. *Hem*: In the same way, pick up 96 sts along the other side of the band and k 3 rounds with purl side out and 2 rnds with k side out. Bind off. Turn hem up and tack down on wrong side.

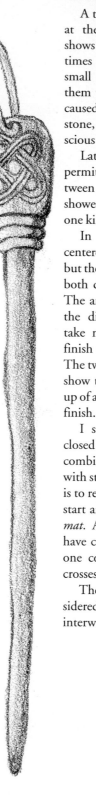

Small braided mats

A tombstone from Hellvi, shown at the beginning of the chapter, shows that the Viking artisan sometimes rounded off the ends of the small mats and other times ended them with points. Perhaps this was caused by the medium, unforgiving stone, or it could have been a conscious aesthetic variation.

Lattice mats in knitted form permit no such fluid transitions between variants. My experiments showed that it is possible to knit only one kind of start or finish at a time.

In the *rounded little knot*, the centered finish (and start) is used, but the *angular little knot* beneath has both directional starts and finishes. The angular version is longer, since the directional starts and finishes take more rows, so the choice of finish affects the size of the motif. The two little knots on the next page show the difference. Both are made up of a start, a single lattice unit and a finish.

I saw different possibilities for closed motifs, depending on how one combined repeats of the lattice unit with starts and finishes. The simplest is to repeat the lattice unit between a start and a finish, as shown in *Little mat*. A corresponding motif could have centered starts and finishes, or one could increase the number of crosses before the finish.

These *little knots* could be considered either short mats or pairs of interwoven rings.

Artifacts and pattern swatches

Above right, a rounded little knot. *The same motif is found on the stylus (facing page) from Slite, Othem parish, Gotland. It is also found on the buckle, top left, from Lousgaard, Bornholm, Denmark.*

The pointy little knot *at center right is also found on a self-buckle from York, England (center, left). The same motif is inscribed in a piece of bone found at Särna, Dalarna (not shown).*

I call the version at the bottom of the page "Motif with a tiny lattice." It is made up of a start, and a finish with two (widthwise) lattice repeats. I used the angular start and finish. If you want a longer motif, simply add more lattice repeats, vertically.

The artifact which inspired it is a "hogback" gravestone from Ingleby Arncliffe, North Yorkshire, England. The original is about a meter wide.

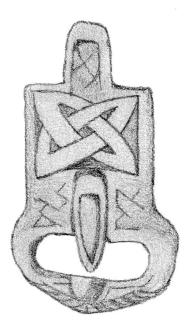

41

Wide lattice and motif

The *wide lattice* is made up of six or more strands interwoven in the same way as the *little lattice*. The repeat can be spread widthwise to become a wider mat or so that it becomes an allover surface pattern. Such a surface pattern decorates the side of a box clasp from Gotland, Sweden.

At top, a little box clasp from Gotland. At center a game board from Balinderry, Ireland, inset with a pattern swatch of wide latticework.

Wide lattices can also be started and finished either centered, directionally, or with a combination of the two.

Centered finish

Mixed finish

Lattice repeat

Mixed start

Centered start

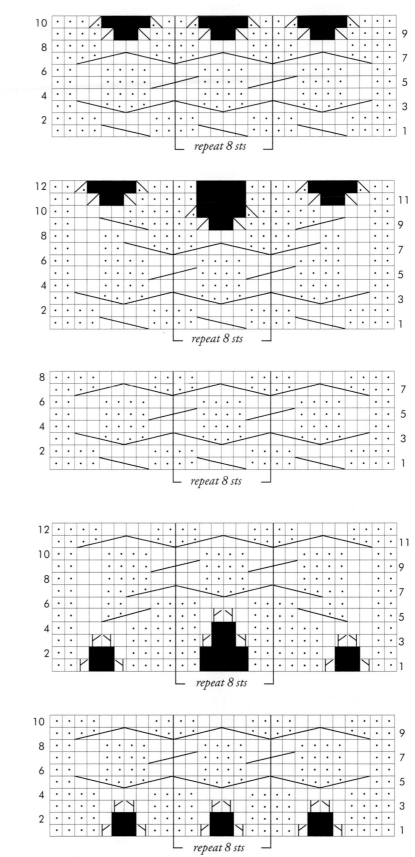

Large Mats

See how the centered finish looks on *rounded mat* below. The motif is found on the shaft of a Viking era cross from England, and, on a medieval Norwegian chair with Viking-like carving, it's found in company with the *rounded little knot*.

Centered finishes or the centered start alone can be used to make horizontal panels or a yoke in lattice pattern. In that case, one simply repeats the lattice unit for the desired number of times for the width of the horizontal pattern. The pattern repeat is shown on all charts.

For the *angular large mat knot*, centered starts and finishes were used in the middle with directional finishes on the outside corners to make a more symmetric motif.

Both knots consist of a start, a lattice unit repeated a number of times, and a finish.

At left: Cross shaft from Kirklevington, Yorkshire, England.

Below: Medieval chair with partially Viking ornamentation from the church at Tyldal, Hedmark, Norway.

Right: Pattern swatches of large mat knot.

Border from Skabersjö

The Skabersjö buckle, with its rich ornamentation, appears now for the third time, here with the pattern I have named after it. Below you can see a magnification of a detail. The whole clasp is shown on p. 50.

When I had analyzed this pattern, I discovered it again on a fragment from Solberga, Sweden, of what must certainly have been a shield ornament.

It's found again on the buckle from Kaupang, Norway, most easily recognizable on the left side, but the pattern on the right seems to be the same, but spaced so much more tightly that it runs together into a common lattice.

The motif in the combined version above right consists of a start and a finish but in the center it's hitched to a cable instead of beginning and ending with centered decreases and increases. To adapt the motif to knitting, the central two strands must be crossed more times than in the original motif to keep the motifs from running into each other.

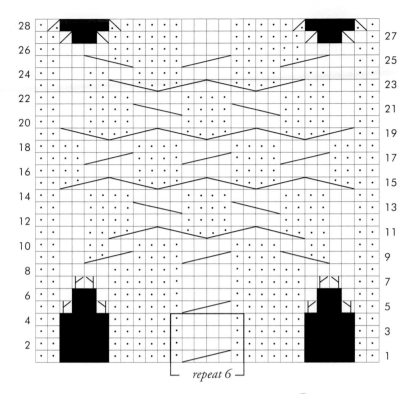

repeat 6

Above and below: Chart for Skabersjö panel pattern swatch.

At right: buckle from Kaupang, Norway

Lower left: Skabersjö buckle with detail of the Skabersjö panel enlarged.

Rafn: the Raven
Jacket with shawl collar and hat

One border of the incredibly rich decoration of the clasp from Skabersjö, Skåne (Sweden) inspired the jacket I call "Rafn." "Rafn" is the old Nordic word for "raven," an intentional contrast between the white and fuzzy alpaca yarn and the shining black raven. The same wonderful yarn is of course used in the matching hat.

Size: S (M) L (XL)

Finished measurements: Bust, about 41/104 (44/112) 47½/120 (50½/128) in/cm. Length about 28¾/73 (29½/75) 30¼/77 (31/79) in/cm. Head measurement, about 30½ in/53 cm.

Materials: 9 (9) 10 (11) 100 g (from Danish version) skeins Alpacka Sport + 2 skeins for cap. 7 buttons, about 1¼ in.

Needles: 3.5 mm and 4 mm; 3.5 and 4 mm circular needles, 40 cm long; and 4 mm double-pointed needles for cap.

Tension: 20 sts and 24 rows in stockinette on 4 mm needles = 4 inches square or 10 x 10 cm. In the knotted panel: 20 sts = 3¼ in/8.5 cm. One motif is approximately 4¼ in/11 cm in length. Make a test swatch, and adjust your needle size up for too many, down for too few sts per 4 in/10 cm. Keep an eye on your tension while knitting.

Pattern: Knitted using chart "Panel from Skabersjö on the preceding page.

Back

On 3.5 mm needles, cast on 111 (119) 127 (135) sts. The first row after the cast-on row is on the wrong side (Ribbing begins and ends with k 1 and the cable in the ribbing starts with row 4 on the chart on p. 45.). Rib in k1, p 1 for 27 (31) 33 (37) sts, k 6 sts in cable following the chart, rib k 1, p 1 for 45 (45) 49 (49) sts, 6 sts cable pattern, and 27 (31) 33 (37) sts ribbing k 1 p 1. Repeat chart Rows 1-4 twice, and Rows 1 + 2 one more time: the ribbing should be 11 rows long. Change to 4 mm needles and knit pattern panel on 20 sts following the chart, placing this directly centered above the two cables in the ribbing and starting with row 3 on the chart. K stockinette on all other sts. When work measures about 19¼/49 (19¾/50) 20/51 (20½/52) in/cm, bind off 2 sts both sides for the armhole and then decrease 1 st each side every other row 8 (10) 12 (14) times = 91 (95) 99 (103) sts. When sleeve hole measures about 9½/24 (9¾/25) 10¼/

26 (10½/27) in/cm, bind off for shoulder 10, 8, 12 (12, 8, 12) 12, 8, 14 (14, 8, 14) sts both sides at the beginning of every row for six rows. Bind off the remaining center 31 sts.

Left front

With 3.5 mm needles, cast on 62 (66) 70 (74) sts. The first row after the cast-on row is on the wrong side of work. (K the first and last st on the armhole side as a selvage st.) Start cable pattern with row 4 on the chart on p. 45. K 29 (29) 31 (31) sts k 1, p 1 ribbing, k 6 sts in cable pattern, k 27 (31) 33 (37) sts in k 1, p 1 ribbing. Continue in this way for 11 rows. Change to 4 mm needles and begin knot pattern on 20 sts, centered on and continuing the cable pattern. Begin with Row 3. K stockinette on remaining sts, except for 9 sts on the front edge: continue these in ribbing. When work measures about 19¼/49 (19¾/50) 20/51 (20½/52) in/cm, shape armhole: Bind off 2 sts on side opposite ribbing, then dec 1 st every second row 8 (10) 12 (14) times. *At the same time*, start the shawl collar and decrease for the neckline: K to 2 sts before the ribbing, SSK, inc1 st to be included in ribbed collar band, rib next 9 sts and cast on a new selvage st, which will be k on both sides of work. Continue to dec for neckline every 4th row 12 times while increasing for shawl collar every other row 30 times (= 41 ribbed sts on collar). When front is as long as back, bind off for shoulder 10, 8, 12 (12, 8, 12) 12, 8, 14 (14, 8, 14) sts at beginning of every second row on armhole side. Continue collar in ribbing. Fill out collar with short rows: Beginning at outer edge of collar, **Rows 1 + 2**: Knit (ribbing) until 5 sts remain, yarn over, turn, and rib back to beginning of row. Note that the first st after the turn must be a k st, to keep the turn invisible. **Rows 3 + 4**: K a short row 4 sts shorter than the previous one, yarn over, turn and rib back. Rib short rows this way, 4 sts shorter each time, until there are no more sts. K (ribbing) all sts, knitting each yarn-over with the st following. (This prevents holes in the work.) Continue to rib until lower

edge of collar is half the width of the back of the neckline. Bind off. Mark positions for 7 buttons, the bottom one in the middle of the lower edge ribbing, the top one at the beginning of the shawl collar incs, the other 5 spaced evenly between them.

Right front
Knit mirror image to the left front, but k buttonholes to match buttonband markings on left front. Bind off 3 sts for each buttonhole, 4 sts in from the front edge, then cast on 3 new sts in the next row. Dec for the neckline by knitting 2 sts together. For the short rows on the collar, k 1 st less before the first yarn-over and turn, in order to make the first st after the turn a k st.

Sleeves
With 3.5 mm needles, cast on 45 (47) 49 (51) sts and rib, k 1, p 1, for 2½ in/6 cm (no cable). The first row = the wrong side of the cuff; begin and end each row with a k (selvage) st. Dec 1 st each end of row once and continue to rib 2 more cm. (The cuff is meant to be turned up.) Change to 4 mm needles and knit in stockinette, Put the pretty side of the cast-on on the purl side of the stockinette, so it will show when the cuff is turned up. Inc 1 st both sides every 6th row 20 (20) 21 (21) times (= 83 (85) 89 (91) sts). When sleeve measures 19 in/48 cm, bind off 2 sts each side for sleeve cap. Dec 1 st each side every second row 8 (10) 12 (14) times. Bind off. Knit another identical sleeve.

Belt
On 3.5 mm needles, cast on 11 sts and rib, k 1, p 1, with a k (selvage) st at both ends, for about 6½ feet/2 meters. Bind off in ribbing.

Assembly
Block all pieces to measure between damp cloths and let the pieces dry completely. Sew shoulder seams. Graft back edges of collar together and tack collar to back neckline. Sew sleeves into armholes, centering top center on shoulder seam. Sew side and underarm seams as one. Sew on buttons. Optionally, crochet loops at sides of waist to receive sash.

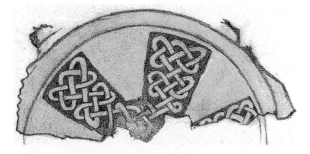

Hat
Note: The directions below are for a tocque, a rounded cap with a wide, erect, turned-up cuff. The hat in the photo, p. 47, was knitted as a tube with curled reverse stockinette edging at the bottom and around the squared crown. The pattern element is too tall for this structure and the hat, as photographed, would slip down over the eyes in use — the probable reason that these directions were substituted.

On 3.5 mm circular needle, cast on 105 sts and k circularly and even for 7 rnds (rounds). Change to 4 mm circular needle and set up 3 panels of pattern, beginning rnd at center back. *K 9 sts, k Skabersjö panel starting on row 2 of chart on p. 45. In each panel, inc 3 sts: 1 st before the cable, 1 st after it, and 1 sts in the middle = 20 sts. K 9 sts.* Knit * - * altogether 3 times = 114 sts. Start on Row 2 of chart and k through once plus repeating Rows 1-3. K 1 rnd. The rest of the cap is in stockinette, but the outside of the crown is the inside of the turned up cuff. To knit rather than purl the rest: Yarn over, turn work inside out and k back the way you came. At the end of the round, k last st together with the yarn-over, to prevent a hole. K 5½ in/14 cm.

Divide work into three equal parts, with a marker at each point and the first marker at center back. Dec: SSK after and k 2 together before each marker every round until 6 sts remain. K even 1 in/2.5 cm, break yarn and draw tail through these sts firmly. Turn up the bottom edge so that the back side of the first stockinette rounds form a little purl sausage on the lower edge.

Pattern sample: Variant of Skabersjö panel

Left: Fragment from Solberga, Östergötland.

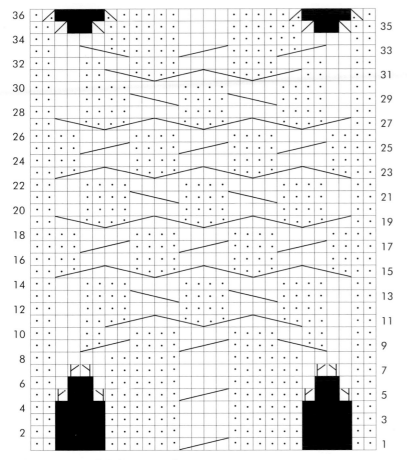

Chart: Variant of Skabersjö panel

Pattern swatches, left to right:
Rhombus on ribbing, rhombus on ribbing with cable, and rhombus

A variant of the Skabersjö panel (lower right, facing page) occurred when I misread the original artifact and recorded an extra repeat in the latticework. The resulting pattern was also pleasing.

However, the three patterns that follow are the result of systematic variation. All three start with the Skabersjö panel and the angular large mat of the variant.

Rhombus on ribbing has six ribs plaited into a rhombus-shaped mat.

Rhombus on ribbing with cable has the two central ribs twisted together into a cable. This is a precursor to the Skabersjö variant, with the corners left open and the strands continuing to form k 2, p 2 ribbing.

The central cable is also found on *Rhombus on cables*, but the two straight inside strands are moved outward and are twisted up with the outermost strand, so that a rhombus lies on three parallel cables.

Buckle from Skabersjö, Skåne, Sweden
The original is 14 cm high. Four of the border patterns have been translated to knitting in this book.

Following the same principle as in the first rhombus pattern, I isolated the "kernel" of the *Little mat* (p. 41) in the following *Narrow panel with little lattice* linking mats with a ribbing pattern. By capping off the central strips, adding a start and a finish to the lattice, the result is a variant of *Ring with interlaced ropes (p. 15).*

In *Wide panel with little lattice,* the outside strips swing out widely between lattices.

Pattern swatch: Narrow panel with little lattice

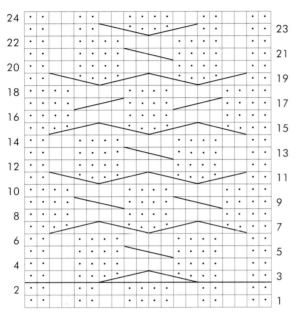

Chart: Narrow panel with little lattice

Chart: Wide panel with little lattice

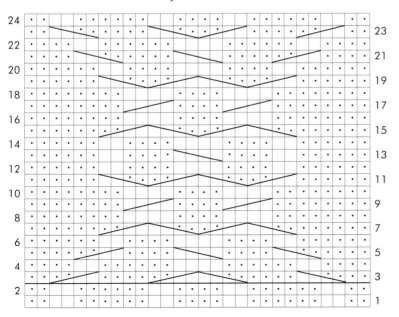

Pattern swatch: Wide panel with little lattice

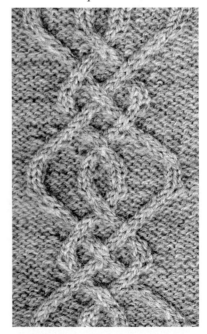

RAGNA
Medieval-look pullover with wide flaps and cap

A handsome pullover with wide flaps at the bottom to evoke thoughts of medieval times. The hat is a becoming finishing touch. The pattern is panels of little framed lattices bordered by ordinary cables that continue unbroken to the neckline and shoulders. The cables are repeated on the sleeves. To knit the sweater without slits in the bottom, simply cast on 160 sts and follow the rest of the directions. If you wish to knit it in another size, read how in "Sizes and Fit" on p. 121.

One size

Finished measurements: Bust, about 47½ in/120 cm. Length, about 27½ in/70 cm. Head circumference, 21½-22½ in/55-57 cm.

Materials: 10 balls Magpie Tweed + 1 ball for cap

Needles: 5 mm needles. 40 cm long 4 mm circular needle for neck.

Tension: 17 sts in stockinette on 5 mm needles = 4 in/10 cm. One pattern motif of 40 sts = 6 in/15 cm. Check your tension carefully, even while knitting the garment.

Back

With 5 mm needles, cast on 40 sts and purl the first row (= wrong side of work) following Row 0 in chart on p. 54 (*Panel with little framed lattice*). Knit Rows 1-16 on the chart for about 6 in/15 cm. K first and last sts as selvage sts. K three more identical pieces. Join these four tabs (= 150 sts) and knit straight up in pattern (knitting the former selvage sts as reverse stockinette) until work measures about 26½ in/68 cm, stopping at the end or the middle of a pattern repeat. Set the center 40 sts on a holder and knit each side separately. Knit 2 rows on each and bind off for shoulders.

Front

Knit like the back until the work is about 24 in/61 cm long, stopping at the end or the middle of a pattern repeat. Set the center 26 sts on a holder and knit each side separately. On the neck side, dec 1 st every other row 7 times. When front is as long as back, bind off shoulders. Repeat mirror-image on the other side.

Sleeves

On 5 mm needles, cast on 50 sts and set up cabled ribbing following chart on p. 54: k 1 (selvage) st. *(k 8 sts right-twisted cable) x 3; *(k 8 sts left twisted cable) x 3*; k selvage st. Knit cabled ribbing for 2¼ in/6 cm. Change to reverse stockinette, except for the 2 center cables, which continue to the shoulder. Inc 1 st each side every 4th row 15 times = 80 sts. When sleeve measures about 17¾ in/45 cm or the desired length, bind off all sts. Knit another identical sleeve.

Assembly

Block all pieces. Sew shoulder seams. With a 4 mm circular needle, pick up 80 sts around the neck and set up cabled ribbing as on cuffs, taking care to continue cables at center front and back: (k 8 sts right-twisted cable) x 3; (k 8 sts left-twisted cable) x 3; then *(k 8 sts right-twisted cable) x 2; (k 8 sts left-twisted cable) x 2. K cabled ribbing for 3 in/8 cm. Bind off in pattern. Sew sleeves in place, matching center top to shoulder seam and allowing 9½ in/25 cm front and back for armhole. Sew underarm and side seams continuously, but leave a slit in each side as long as the other slits (about 6 in/15 cm).

Cap

With 5 mm needles, cast on 28 sts and knit pattern (center chart on p. 54) for about 21½ in/55 cm (5 whole repeats) with two k (selvage) sts each side. Bind off tightly. *Crown*: Pick up 90 sts along one side and k flat: On back of work, k 1 row, increasing 8 sts, evenly distributed ([k 11, make 1] x 8), inside the selvage sts (= 98 sts). Purl 1 row, k 1 row. These three purl rows (on outside of work) are the beginning of the crown. Place markers dividing the sts into 8 equal groups of 12 sts each, and k stockinette 4 rows.

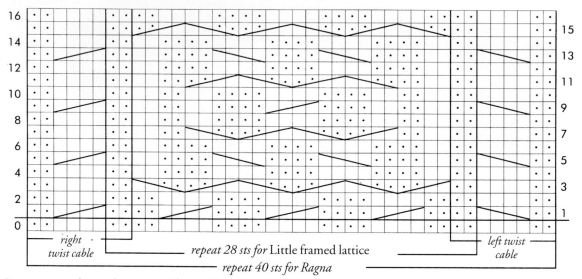

right twist cable   *left twist cable*

repeat 28 sts for Little framed lattice

repeat 40 sts for Ragna

Decrease row: knit selvage st, *After each marker, SSK; before each marker, k 2 together,* Repeat * - * across row, knit selvage st. Dec in this way every 4th row until 16 sts remain. K 2 together across row = 8 sts. Break yarn and draw tail through these sts.

Assembly
Sew sides together and pull so the seam lies flat. Sew crown using *seam stitch,* p. 118.

In the following panel, I've worked two more strands into *Narrow panel with small lattice.* This pattern borders yet another box clasp recovered on Gotland. On this clasp, the little lattice is cut free from the center band. It wasn't possible to do this in knitting without completely changing the character of the pattern, but this version is the closest possible in knitting. Two more panels follow, that in principle are two halves of *Panel with little framed lattice* but with the right and left half offset rhythmically. In the second of these, the outside strand swings outward widely. Both panels can be effectively mirrored by knitting one of a pair starting with row 17; the other, with row 1.

Chart for Ragna and Panel with little framed lattice

Pattern swatch of Panel with little framed lattice

A box clasp from Gotland, the source for Panel with little framed lattice, *has a similar but not identical ornamentation.*

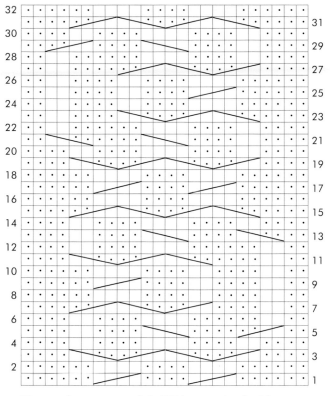

Chart and pattern swatch for Wide serpentine braid

Pattern swatch and chart for Narrow serpentine braid

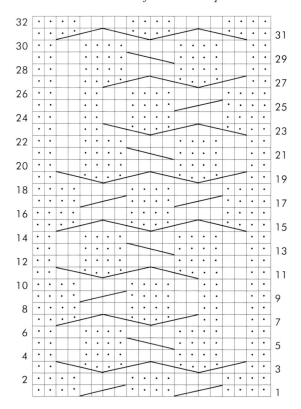

FRODE

Pullover with happiness sign and serpentine braids

The St. John's cross as a pre-Christian symbol of happiness has already been described in "Rings and Chains" and nothing's wrong with knitting it into a sweater in hope of good fortune. The sweater is simplicity itself, the shape accentuated by the interplay of the large, stable St. John's crosses and the mobile, serpentine panels of braiding.

Sizes: XS (S) M (L) XL

Finished measurements: Bust, 37¾/96 (40/100) 42½/108 (44/112) 46½/118 in/cm. Length, 21/53 (22/56) 23/59 (23½/60) 25/63 in/cm.

Materials: 12 (13) 14 (15) 17 skeins Smart.

Needles: 3.5 mm and 4 mm needles, 40 cm long 3.5 mm circular needle.

Tension: 20 sts and 28 rows in stockinette on 4 mm needles = 4 inches square or 10 cm x 10 cm. Check your tension before starting.

Pattern: Knit following chart for *Wide serpentine braid* (p. 55) and *Large St. John's Cross* (p. 31). One *wide serpentine braid* begins on Row 1; the other on Row 17, which makes them mirror each other.

Front

With 3.5 mm needles, cast on 110 (114) 122 (126) 134 sts and rib: k 2, p 2, for 1½ in/4 cm. Change to 4 mm needles and purl 12 (12) 16 (16) 20 sts (reverse stockinette), k 2, start chart for *wide serpentine braid* (24 sts) at Row 17 (including 2 incs, one on each side of crossing strands); k 2, p 34 (38) 38 (42) 42 sts (reverse stockinette), k 2, start chart for *wide serpentine braid* at Row 1 (including 2 incs, one on each side of crossing strands = 24 sts); k 2 and p 12 (12) 16 (16) 20 sts. **Note:** Start on the front side of work (check that the pretty side of cast-on row is on the same side). In this first pattern row, you have increased 2 sts in each panel of braid (1 st on each side of the crosses) = 114 (118) 126 (130) 138 sts. After 6 (8) 10 (10) 12 rows, knit a *Large happiness sign* (chart p. 31) dead center on the reverse stockinette panel, then k 6 (8) 10 (10) 12 more rows reverse stockinette and k another *Large happiness sign*. Repeat this sequence, and after the third *Large happiness sign*, k 6 (8) 10 (10) 12 rows, and put the center 20 (22) 22 (24) 24 sts on a holder and k each side separately, decreasing 1 st at neck edge every other row 5

times. When work measures about 21/53 (22/56) 23½/59 (23½/60) 25/63 in/cm, bind off shoulder sts.

Back

Knit just like the front, but after the last central cross, knit in reverse stockinette until work is ¾ in/2 cm short of its final length. Place the center 28 (30) 30 (32) 32 sts on a holder and knit each side separately. Dec a single st on each neck edge and k shoulder, in pattern, until they're as long as front. Bind off.

Sleeves

On 3.5 mm needles, cast on 42 (46) 46 (50) 50 sts and rib, k 2, p 2 for 1½ in/4 cm. Change to 4 mm needles, knit reverse stockinette, increasing 1 st each side every fourth row 25 (25) 27 (27) 29 times = 92 (96) 100 (104) 108 sts. When sleeve measures about 19 in/48 cm, bind off. Knit another identical sleeve.

Assembly

Block all pieces. Sew the shoulder seams. *Neckband:* With 3.5 mm circular needle, pick up 86 (90) 90 (98) 98 sts around the neck and k circularly in k 2 p 2 ribbing for 2 in/5 cm. Bind off in ribbing. Sew sleeves in, matching center of sleeve top to shoulder seam and allowing 9/23 (9½/24) 9¾/25 (10¼/26) 10½/27 in/cm on each side for armhole. Sew side and underarm seams as one seam.

Running Knots

I've called this group of patterns "running knots," as they are in various forms a single strand knotted over itself. They could also be called "self-knots." The simplest of them looks like a pretzel, but variations on the theme abound. The overhand knot is widespread, both in form and in geographic area.

Many representations of Viking women seem to show them with a knot tied in their hair, as seen in the minute "guldgubber" ("golden guys" or "golden old men") find on Ekerö, Sweden.

Guldgubber, about the size of a thumbnail, on foil-thin sheets of goldleaf, are from the Vandal era, that preceded the age of the Vikings. Vandal artisans clearly set their stamp on Viking ornamentation. In this "golden granny's" hair is the simplest overhand knot one can imagine.

On a little metal plate from Lousgaard, Bornholm, Denmark, the overhand knot itself is just as simple, but repeated and more artistically represented.

Often the knots follow one another in rows, as on this little horse-like figure from Birka (Sweden).

Above left: Guldgubbe from Helgö, Uppland, Sweden

Right: Metal plate from Lousgaard, Bornholm, Denmark

Left: Horse (?) from Birka, Uppland

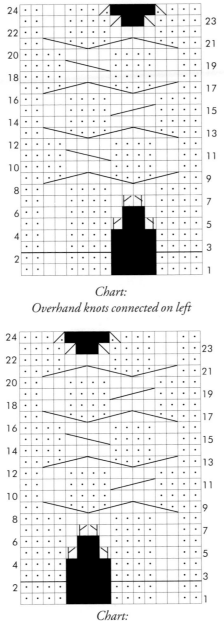

Chart:
Overhand knots connected on left

Chart:
Overhand knots connected on right

Pattern swatch: Overhand knots
connected on left

Pattern swatch: Overhand knots
connected on right

As a knitting motif, the overhand knot is shown in two simple, mirrored versions, one with the connecting line on the left, the other with it on the right.

On a metal plate from Vendel (Sweden), the left and right connecting lines are laid up like a zipper mad was on a dagger sheath from Valsgärde (Sweden).

metal plate from Vendel, Uppland

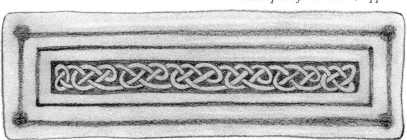

Overhand knots in zipperlike left and right facing columns. On this page, chart and pattern swatch for a rounded version; on the facing page, chart and pattern swatch for an angular variant. To make a mirror image, start on Row 23 (rounded) or Row 25 (angular).

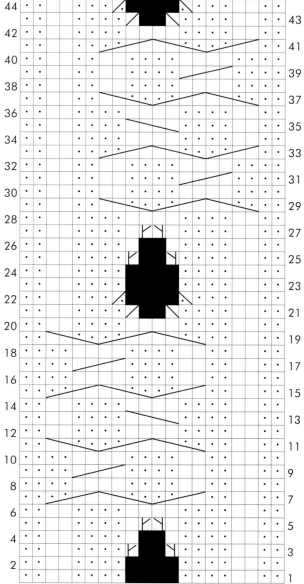

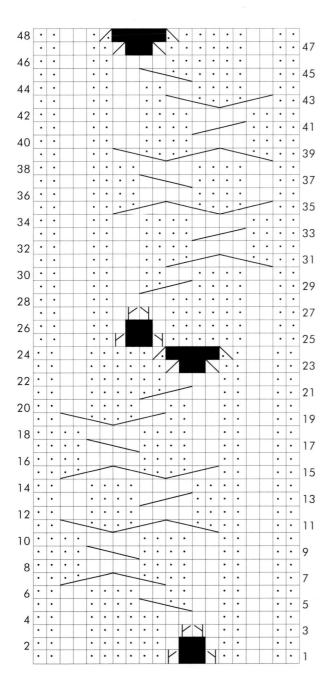

The sheath was in such poor condition that I couldn't be sure it was a zigzag row of overhand knots, but I have taken it for such. The overhand knot is also shown below in an angular version which gives a clearer impression of how it works. These two panels can also be flipped mirror-image, by beginning one of a pair on Row 15 of the chart.

I've come across many examples of two zigzag lines of mirrored knots crossing one another. The shield plate from Valsgärde has an intriguing border that begins with a plaited mat, continues with paired, crossing overhand knots, and ends with the Skabersjö panel.

Pattern swatch: Angular zigzag overhand knots

Pattern swatch: Zigzag overhand knots

Chart: Zigzag overhand knots

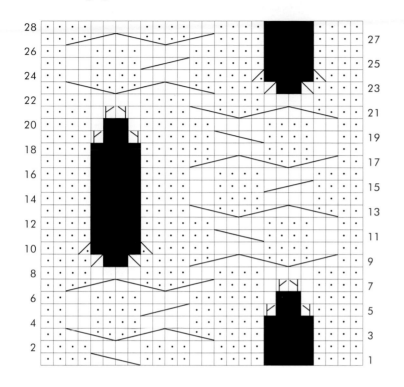

Chart: Angular zigzag overhand knots

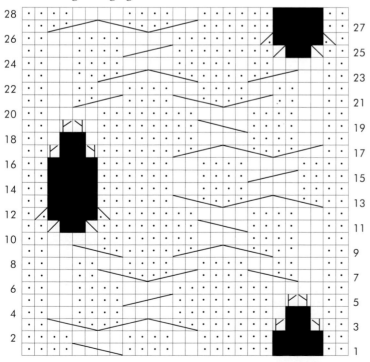

*Knife sheath from Valsgärde,
Uppland, Sweden*

*Shield plate from
Valsgärde,
Uppland, Sweden*

VEBJÖRG
Tailored cardigan with overhand knots

Two opposite panels with mirrored overhand knots catch the eye, effectively accenting the cardigan's feminine shaping. The pattern follows the button bands and neckline and, by knitting around the corner, becomes a patterned yoke on the back.

Sizes: S (M) L

Finished measurements: Bust, 36¼/92 (39¼/100) 42½/108 in/cm. Length, 28½ in/73 cm.

Materials: 6 (6) 7 balls Yllets Ullgarn 3. 7 buttons.

Needles: 3.5 mm and 4 mm.

Tension: 20 sts x 26 rows in stockinette on 4 mm needles = 4 inches square or 10 x 10 cm. 1 pattern repeat = 2¼ in/6 cm wide x 3½ in/9 cm long. Check your tension carefully before starting any project.

Note: This cardigan is knitted in 7 pieces: back, left and right fronts, 2 sleeves, and 2 pattern panels that continue around to form the yoke, where they are sewn together.

Back

On 3.5 mm needles, cast on 93 (101) 109 sts and rib: p 1, k 1 for 9 rows. Be sure to have 1 k st at both ends on right side of work inside the k 1 (selvage) st. Change to 4 mm needles and k stockinette st. After 4/10 (3/8) 2½/6 in/cm, dec 1 st each side every 6th row 5 times, then every 4th row 4 (5) 6 times = 75 (81) 87 sts. When work measures about 13¾/35 (13¾/34) 13/33 in/cm, inc 1 st each side every 4th row 9 (10) 11 times = 93 (101) 109 sts. When work measures about 20½/53 (20½/52) 20/51 in/cm, bind off for armhole: 3, 2 (4, 3) 5, 4 sts each side, then dec 1 st each side every other row 4 (5) 6 times = 75 (77) 79 sts. When work measures about 23½ in/60 cm, bind off the center 65 sts and work each side separately. When the armholes measure 8¼/21 (8½/22) 9/23 in/cm, bind off the remaining 5 (6) 7 sts for the shoulder.

Left side/front

With 3.5 mm needles, cast on 27 (31) 35 sts and rib, p 1, k 1 for 9 rows. Remember the k1 selvage st at both ends, and be sure to have a k st on the front of the work at both ends just inside the selvage st. Change to 4 mm needles and knit in stockinette st. Dec and inc on the armhole side (only!) as directed above for the back. When the work measures about 20¾/53 (20½/52) 20/51 in/cm, begin decs for neckline and armholes. On the armhole side, bind off the same number of sts as on the back and *at the*

same time dec at the front edge by SSK just inside the selvage st, every 4th row, 13 times. When armhole measures 8¼/21 (8½/22) 9/23 in/cm, bind off remaining 5 (6) 7 sts for shoulder.

Right side/front

Knit mirror image to left front. Dec on front edge by k 2 together just inside the selvage st.

Left front pattern panel

With 3.5 mm needles, cast on 31 sts and k pattern following *Chart 1 left* on p. 66, the first 5 rows following Row 0, then repeating Rows 1-24. After 9 rows, change to 4 mm needles. After 7 entire repeats + 22 rows of the 8th repeat, place a marker on the outer edge for the shoulder (on the fabric, not the needle). K 1 repeat following *diagram 2 left,* then another following *diagram 1 left* but beginning at Row 5. Bind off all sts. Place markers for 7 buttons, the lowest in the middle of bottom ribbing, the top at the beginning of the V-neck decs (about 20¾/53 (20¾/52) 20/51 in/cm from the bottom edge), and distributing the rest evenly between them.

Right front pattern panel

Knit mirror image to the left but with buttonholes corresponding to the button markings on the left. For each buttonhole, bind off 2 sts, 3 sts from front edge, then cast on 2 sts in the next row. For pattern directions, follow *diagrams 1* and *2 right* on p. 67.

Sleeves

On 3.5 mm needles, cast on 43 (45) 47 sts and rib, p 1, k1, for 9 rows. Include a k selvage st and, at both edges, 1 k st on the front of work inside selvage st. Change to 4 mm needles and stockinette st. Inc 1 st each side every 4th row 15 times = 73 (75) 77 sts. When sleeve measures about 17 in/43 cm, bind off 4 sts for the sleeve cap on both sides. Then dec 1 st each side, every other row until 25 sts remain. Bind off 2 sts at the beginning of every row 6 times. Bind off the remaining 13 sts. K another identical sleeve.

Chart 1 left

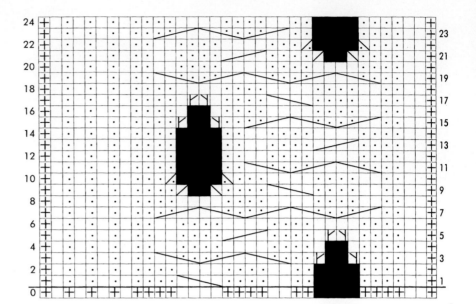

Chart 2 left

Assembly

Block all pieces to measure between damp cloths and let them dry completely. Sew the (tiny) shoulder seams, and sew the yoke together at center back. I used a "false grafting st" through the bound-off sts, which creates a pretty seam down the back. Pin the front pattern panel with the marker about ½ in/1 cm behind the shoulder seam, matching center back to center back and the corners set firmly into the corners of the back cutaway. Sew the front panels to the side/fronts and back with st seams, inside the selvage sts. Sew the underarm and side seams as one. Sew the sleeves into the armholes. Sew on the buttons.

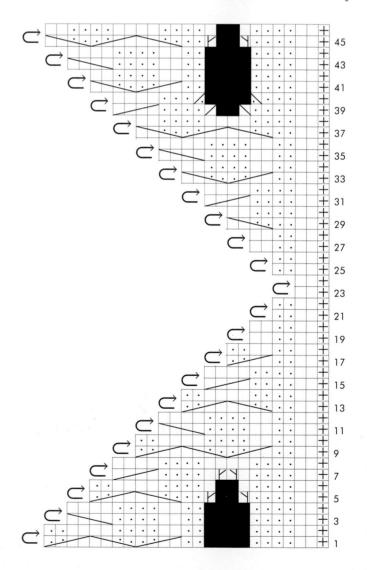

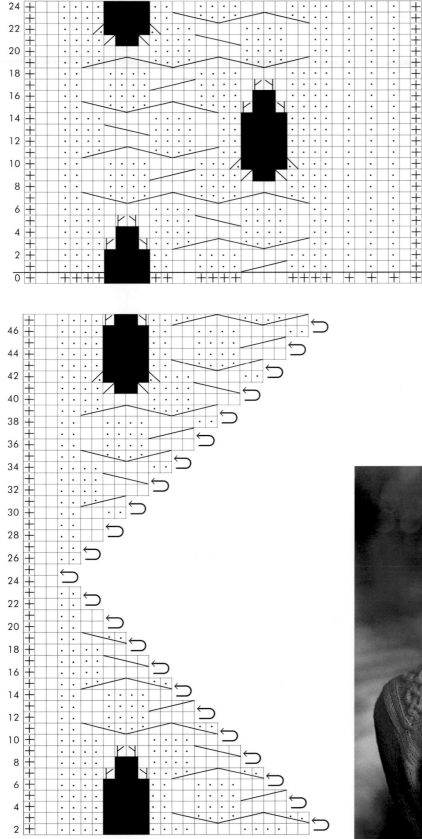

Chart 1 right

Chart 2 right

Top: *Picture stone from floor of Alskogs Kyrka, Gotland, Sweden*

Below: *Sword hilt (the "crown" of the handle) from Valsgärde, Uppland, Sweden*

One of the smartest renditions of overhand knots in a crossing zigzag is on the picture stone at left from Alskogs Church on Gotland (Sweden). The disfiguring hole occurred because the stone was mortared into the floor of the church underneath the baptismal font. The hole was bored for drainage!

On a sword hilt from Valsgärde (Sweden), a variant of the pattern is seen with an extra crossover between repeats. As the Valsgärde sword hilt is in itself a whole exploration of Viking ornamentation, I have for clarity's sake enlarged the relevant band of pattern.

The sword hilt seems also to be damaged (on the right edge), but in this case, it is the photographer, or the copyist, who is to blame. The hilt itself is intact.

The little animal figure from Södermanland on the facing page is also in perfect condition, although it's not at all clear *which* species of animal it represents.

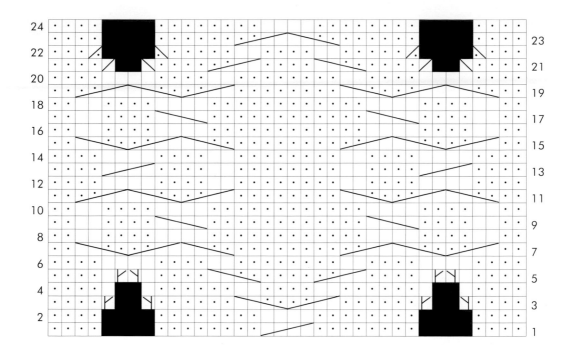

Above and right: Chart and pattern swatch of overhand knots in a crossing zigzag

Below left: Animal figure from Löta, Bettna parish, Södermanland

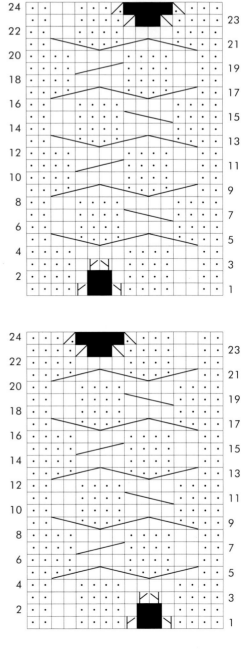

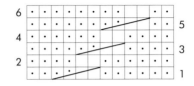

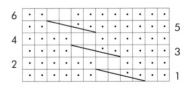

Pattern swatches: Figure eight knot, left and right

Charts, starting at top:
Right figure-eight
Left figure-eight
Right diagonal
Left diagonal

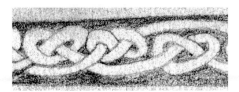

Metal plate from Vendel, detail.

Pattern swatches and charts: angular figure eight knot. The top chart is for the right pattern swatch.

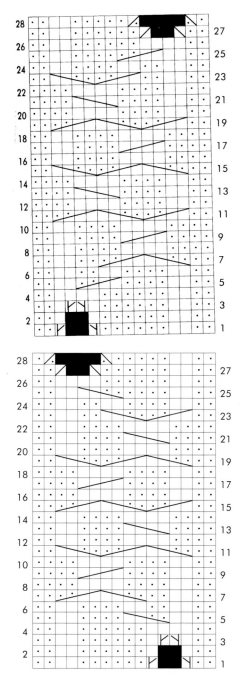

The last pattern in this group is a "double overhand knot," that is, an overhand knot where one bight of the knot has been twisted and one tail drawn through the resulting loop. This is generally called a "figure eight knot" in nautical parlance. A simple one is found surrounded by ordinary overhand knots on the metal plate from Vendel. Was it a mistake or could it have been an intentional variation?

It differs from the simple overhand knot in that the figure of eight knot begins and ends on opposite sides of the panel. This can be useful as a centrally/placed motif, but to knit a long panel, one has to shift the knot from right- to left-handed knots or bring the strand diagonally back to the side where it started. The chart for left and right diagonal connectors has that function. Both a rounded and an angular version are shown here, and both are charted for right and left handed knots. The charts of diagonals on the facing page can be used for either.

S-Hitches from Ardre

The "S" shape appears in various forms in many cultures. It is found in pre-Columbian South American textiles, on Coptic stockings from 1200 AD, and in a vast array of Celtic patterns. In the Estonian textile tradition it represents the snake or serpent, and it's easy to assume that it meant the same in the Nordic representational idiom.

The Vikings integrated the "S" into their braided ornamentation. I ran across it first on the edge of a Gotland picture stone from Ardre—thus the name—but it also appears on other picture stones in Gotland, including the one shown here from Bota in Garda parish.

The panel shows up with variations on a pendant from the Norwegian treasure find at Hon.

The motif is made up of two strands that alternate in moving from side to side and being slung around the other in the shape of an S (or a backward S). You can see this clearly in the diagram at right.

I haven't run into many examples

Right: Picture stone from Bota, Garda parish, Gotland.

Below: Little pendant from Hon, Norway

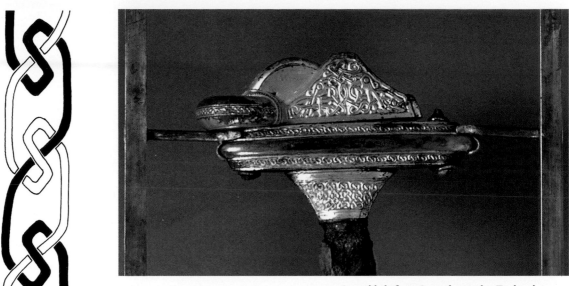

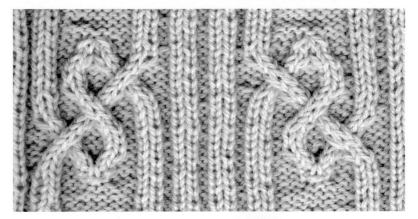

Sword hilt from Pappilanmäki, Finland.

from Finland, so it is with special pleasure that I show the Ardre S-hitches on the magnificent sword hilt from Pappilanmäki, Finland, above.

The pattern swatches and charts show the motif in both right and left twisted versions.

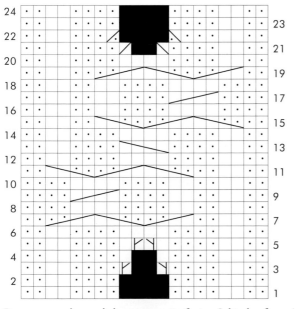

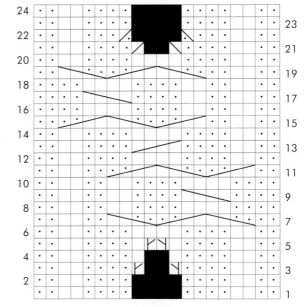

Pattern swatches and charts: opposite facing S-hitches from Ardre

HARALD

Pullover, watch cap, socks, and mittens with S-hitches

Harald is shaped like a classic fisherman's guernsey. The unadorned bottom half of the sweater saved work: originally, that part of the sweater was covered by the fisherman's workpants. The smooth surfaces balance the intricate patterning that results from laying mirrored panels of the S-hitch from Ardre side by side across the entire yoke.

The cap, mittens, and socks are very simply knit. The cap is a tube with some decreases at the top, the socks are tubes with a toe and the heel added later, using the same decrease pattern as on the toe. The mittens are knit on the same lines, with shaping only at the tips.

Sizes: Unisex S (M) L

Finished measurements: chest, 42½/108 (46½/118) 50/127 in/cm. Length, 27/69 (28¼/72) 29½/75 in/cm.

Materials: 9 (9) 10 skeins Lord of Aran.

Needles: 4.5 mm and 5 mm.

Tension: 17 sts x 23 rows in stockinette on 5 mm needles = 4 inches square or 10 x 10 cm. Check your tension carefully. Make a swatch before and continue to check as you knit.

Back

On 4.5 mm needles, cast on 94 (102) 110 sts and knit ribbing, p 2, k 2, for 3 in/8 cm. (The first row starts on the wrong side of the work and should begin and end with 2 p sts.) Change to 5 mm needles and knit stockinette. When work measures 14½/37 (15¼/39) 16/41 in/cm, begin the yoke: Starting on front of work, K 2 rows, p 1 row, and k 2 rows, and on the last k row, inc 8 (12) 12 sts evenly distributed over the row = 102 (114) 122 sts. P 1 row and begin to follow the chart, starting at the point marked for your size (**Size S:** k *a* twice, **Size L:** K Rows 1 + 2 an extra time between repeats.) K 3 repeats of the chart. Put the center 30 sts on a holder and k each side separately. Repeat Rows 1 + 2 twice and dec at the same time 2 sts at the neck edges, only once. Bind off shoulders.

Front

K like the back for 2 repeats + 2 rows. Place the center 14 sts on a holder and k each side separately. Dec at neck edge every other row, first 2 sts twice, then 1 st 6 times. Bind off shoulder sts at the same height as the back.

Sleeves

On 4.5 mm needles, cast on 42 (42) 46 sts and knit ribbing, p 2, k 2 for 4 in/10 cm. The first row is on wrong side of work, so begin and end with p 2 so that you will have 2 k sts at both ends on the right side of work. Change to 5 mm needles, stockinette st, and inc 4 (6) 4 sts evenly spaced across row = 46 (48) 50 sts. Be sure that the pretty side of the cast-on sts is on the p side of the stockinette, as the cuffs are meant to be turned up. Inc 1 st each side every 4th row 19 (20) 21 times = 84 (88) 92 sts. When work measures 19½ in/50 cm for women or 21¼ in/54 cm for men, k 2 rows, p 2 rows and bind off all sts. K an identical second sleeve.

Assembly

Block all pieces to measurements, lay damp cloths over and let everything dry completely. Sew the right shoulder seam. *Neckband:* On 4.5 mm needles, pick up 90 sts around the neck and p 1 row, k 2 rows, p 1 row, k 2 rows. Dec 8 sts, evenly distributed over the last k row and then p 1 row. Rib k 2 p 2 for 2¼ in/6 cm, being careful to have 2 k sts on both ends on the right side of work. Bind off in ribbing. Sew the left shoulder seam and the side of the neck. Turn in the neck and tack to sts on the wrong side. Sew in sleeves, matching center top to shoulder seam and allowing 26 cm each side for the armhole. Sew underarm and side seams continuously.

Watch cap (or, Grunge Cap) with S-hitches on crown
Finished measurements: around head, 21½-22¾ in/55-58 cm.
Materials: One skein Lord of Aran
Needles: One 40 cm long 4.5 mm circular needle. A set of 4.5 mm double-pointed needles.
Tension: 18 sts in stockinette on 4.5 mm needles = 4 inches or 10 cm. Check your tension carefully and adjust needle size accordingly.
Note: Cap is knitted circularly.

With 4.5 mm circular needle, cast on 96 sts and rib k 2, p 2 for 6¼ in/16 cm. Decrease as follows, changing to double-pointed needles as needed: *k 2, p 1, p 2 together, p 4, p 2 together, p 1, k 2, p 2* and repeat around = 84 sts. *At the same time*, begin chart at bottom of this page, knitting it only once. After completing chart, dec as follows: *k 2, p 2 together, p 1, k 2, p 1, p 2 together, k 2, p 2* and repeat around = 72 sts. Rib, k 2, p 2 for 6 rnds. Dec on the next rnd: *k 2, p 2 together* all the way around, then k 1 rnd without decreases. *K 1 SSK around. K 1 rnd with no decs. K 2 together around for the next 2 rnds. Break yarn and pull it through the remaining sts.

Mittens with S-hitched cuffs
Sizes: Women's (Men's) Medium
Materials: 2 skeins Lord of Aran
Needles: 1 set of five 4 mm double-pointed needles.
Tension: 20 sts x 26 rnds in stockinette on 4 mm needles = 4 inches square or 10 x 10 cm.

Cuff: On 4 double-pointed 4 mm needles, cast on 56 sts, and knit around, following pattern on chart below. K only one repeat in height. **Right Hand:** Change to stockinette st and dec 4 (3) sts per needle = 40 (44) sts. K 2¾/7 (3/8) in/cm and place thumb marker: K the first 7 (8) sts with a contrasting yarn, then back up and reknit these sts with working yarn and continue knitting around until hand measures 3½/9 (4/10.6) in/cm. *Dec for top*: K 2 sts together at the end of the 4th needle and SSK at the beginning of the first needle. Repeat this at the end of the 2nd and beginning of the 3rd needles. Dec in this way every other rnd until 12 sts remain. Break yarn and pull tail through remaining sts. *Thumb:* Carefully pick out the waste yarn marking the thumb hole, distribute the 14 (16) sts on 4 needles, and knit around for 2/5 (2¾/6.5) in/cm. Dec in the same way as on the hand until 8 sts remain. Break yarn and pull tail through remaining sts. K second mitten with the thumb on the last 7 (8) sts of 2nd needle.

Chart below is used for all Harald designs

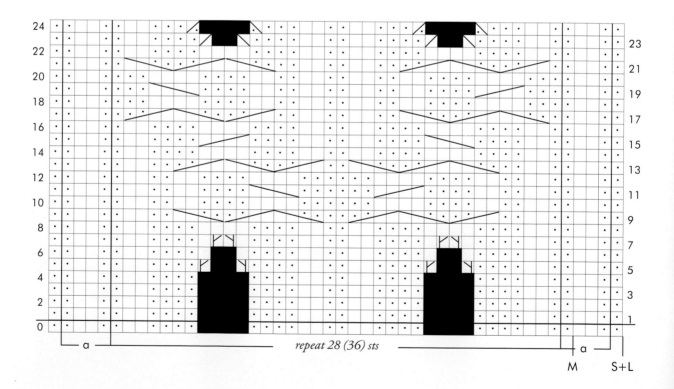

Socks with S-hitched pattern on cuff

Sizes: Women's (Men's) Medium.

Materials: 2 skeins Lord of Aran.

Needles: One set of 5 double-pointed 4 mm needles.

Tension: 20 sts in stockinette on 4 mm needles = 4 inches or 10 cm. Watch your tension closely and adjust needle size if you're off.

Note: The socks are knitted circularly as a tube with the heel added afterwards.

Cuff: On 4 double-pointed 4 mm needles, cast on 56 sts and k around, following chart on p. 76. K 2 repeats. *Foot*: Change to stockinette and dec 3 (2) sts per needle in the first rnd (= 44 (48) sts). *Mark heel* position: K the first and last needles with a contrasting color yarn (= 22 (24) sts). Go back and reknit these sts with working yarn and continue in stockinette until the foot measures 5¼/14 (6¼/16) in/cm. *Dec for toe*: K 2 together at the end of the first needle and SSK at the beginning of the 2nd. Repeat this at the end of the 3rd and the beginning of the 4th needle. Dec in this way every other rnd until 16 sts remain. Graft the top and bottom of the toe together. *Heel:* Carefully remove the contrasting yarn and distribute the 44 (48) sts onto 4 needles, with the first and 4th needle on the sole of the foot. Dec in the same way as on the toe, then graft the top and bottom together. Knit another, identical sock.

VIGDIS
Tunic with separate hood

A cuddly, generously-sized tunic, lovely to crawl into on a cold winter evening or a crisp fall day. The back is extra long but if you wish, you can knit it the same length front and back.

The hood is perfect winter headwear, and the backpack is a stylish accessory. The motif is the S-hitch from Ardre, tightly plaited.

Sizes: S (M) L

Finished measurements: Bust, 45½/116 (50¼/128) 55/140 in/cm. Front length, 31¾/81 (33/84) 33½/85 in/cm; back length, 37¾/96 (38½/98) 39/100 in/cm.

Materials: 12 (13) 15 balls Chunky Tweed + 2 balls for hood and 3 balls for backpack. 1 button and a shackle for backpack.

Needles: Tunic: 5.5 mm and 6.5 mm. 40 cm long 5.5 mm circular needle. Hood: 40 cm long 5.5 mm and 6.5 mm circular needles. Backpack: 60 cm long 5.5 mm and 6.5 mm circular needles.

Tension: 13 sts x 18 rows in stockinette st on 6.5 mm needles = 4 inches square or 10 x 10 cm. Pattern panel's 40 sts = 9¾ inches/25 cm. Keep a close watch on your tension and adjust needle size accordingly.

Pattern: Knit following chart for *S-Hitch from Ardre with Cables* (p. 81) and chart for right and left twisted cables (p. 80).

Front

With 5.5 mm needles, cast on 92 (100) 108 sts. Set up pattern (Start on wrong side of work and place markers if needed): 8 sts for *left twisted cable*; 17 (21) 25 sts p 1, k 1 ribbing; 8 sts for right twisted cable, 9 sts of p 1, k 1 ribbing; 8 sts for right twist cable; 9 sts p 1 k 1 ribbing; 8 sts left twist cable; 17 (21) 25 sts p 1 k 1 ribbing; 8 sts for right twist cable. **Note:** K 2 selvage sts at both edges instead of the 2 p sts indicated on the chart for the first 6 in/15 cm, thereafter 1 selvage st (This marks slit). After 9 rows, change to 6.5 mm needles and continue cables, but start *S-hitch* pattern following chart on the center 24 sts and k stockinette over the 17 (21) 25 sts previously ribbed on each side. K 6 repeats of the chart (30 in/76 cm). Place the center 14 sts on a holder and k each side separately. On the neck edges, dec 1 st every 2nd row 5 times. Bind off for shoulders when work measures 32/81 (33/84) 33½/85 in/cm.

Back

K like the front but for 7 repeats of the chart (34½ in/88 cm). **Note:** K 11¾ in/30 cm with 2 knitted selvage sts on each side, thereafter with 1 selvage st. Place the center 24 sts on a holder and k each side separately. K 4 more rows and bind off shoulders.

Sleeves

With 5.5 mm needles, cast on 31 (33) 35 sts and rib: p1, k 1 for 2½ in/7 cm. Change to 6.5 mm needles, k stockinette st and inc 1 st each side every 4th row 16 times = 63 (65) 67 sts. When sleeve measures 17¼/44 (17/43) 16½/42 in/cm, bind off. K another identical sleeve.

Assembly

Block all pieces. Sew shoulder seams. Neckband: On a 5.5 mm circular needle, pick up 78 sts around the neck and rib, k 1, p 1, except at center front and center back, continue the end of the cable, for 4 in/10 cm. Bind off in pattern. Sew sleeves in, matching center with shoulder seam and allowing 9½/24 (9¾/25) 10¼/26 in/cm front and back for armhole. Sew side and underarm seams continuously but leave the side bottom open where there are 2 selvage sts (6 in/15 cm in front and 11¾/30 cm in back).

Hood

On 5.5 mm circular needle, cast on 70 sts and k around in k 1, p 1 ribbing for 6 in/15 cm. Put 10 center front sts on a holder, change to 6.5 mm circular needle and k stockinette back and forth on the needle. Dec 1 st each side every 2nd row three times. K even until work measures 12½ in/32 cm. Mark center back and dec on both sides of marker: K 3 sts together 3 sts before marker; k 3 sts twisted together 2 sts after marker every 2nd row 5 times. Next row, k to 3 sts before marker, SSK (2 sts only), k 2, k 2 together, and on the next right side row, SSK before the marker and k 2 together after it. K together while binding off: At the marker, divide

the work onto 2 needles with the points facing the face (front) edge. With right sides facing, k 2 sts together (one from each needle) binding off as you do so. On 5.5 mm circular needle, pick up 80 sts around the face opening and k around in stockinette for 1¼ in/3 cm. Bind off. Turn this edge inside and tack to inside of hood.

Backpack

On 5.5 mm circular needle, cast on 96 sts and k around in k 2 p 2 ribbing for 8 rnds. Knit holes for drawstring on 9th rnd: Begin in the middle of a k rib *SSK, double yarn over (wrap yarn twice around needle), k 2 together.* Repeat * - * around. Change to 6.5 mm circular needle and k stockinette st (In the double yarn overs, k 1 p 1 in the first rnd.). When work measures 14½ in/36 cm, p 3 rnds to mark the edge of the bottom. Divide work in 4 parts, 2 short sides of 16 sts each and 2 long sides of 32 sts each. Place markers at each corner. Dec: Beginning at a marker, *SSK, k to 2 sts before the next marker, k 2 together*. Repeat * - * at each corner until the sts for the short sides are used up. Place remaining sts on 2 needles, with the points facing the front edge. With right sides of work facing, k 2 (one from each needle) sts together across row and bind off at the same time. *Pocket*: on 6.5 mm needles, cast on 32 sts and k the entire chart on p. 81, replacing the outermost 2 p sts at both ends with 2 k selvage sts. K rows 1 and 2 twice, then the entire chart, then rows 1 and 2 twice. Finally, k rows 1 and 2, substituting k stockinette for the p stockinette sts. Bind off in pattern. Crochet a little button loop above the center cable.

Assembly

Sew on pocket with the lower edge along one long side of the bottom. Sew a button opposite the button loop. Cut 4 lengths of yarn 18¾ ft/6 m long and twist a cord. Knot the ends, allowing the yarn to fluff into a tassel. Pull the cord through the knitted holes starting at center front so it can be tied in front. Pull the cord out at center back to form shoulder strap. Sew shackle to the middle of the cord, and a corresponding loop to the bottom of the back pack. Optionally, stiffen the bottom with cardboard or stiff plastic and line with a firm fabric.

Pattern swatch on this and the facing page show variants of S-Hitch from Ardre on cables. The charts below are referred to in the directions.

Here I've cabled together mirrored bands of S-hitches. On the left, the pattern is knitted as a panel, following the center 24 sts of the chart. As the outer strands have nothing to twist around, I've knitted them plain. The pattern swatch at right shows the center panel repeated as an allover pattern, while the swatch at the bottom of opposite page shows the panel with the outer cables included, that is, knitted according to the entire chart below.

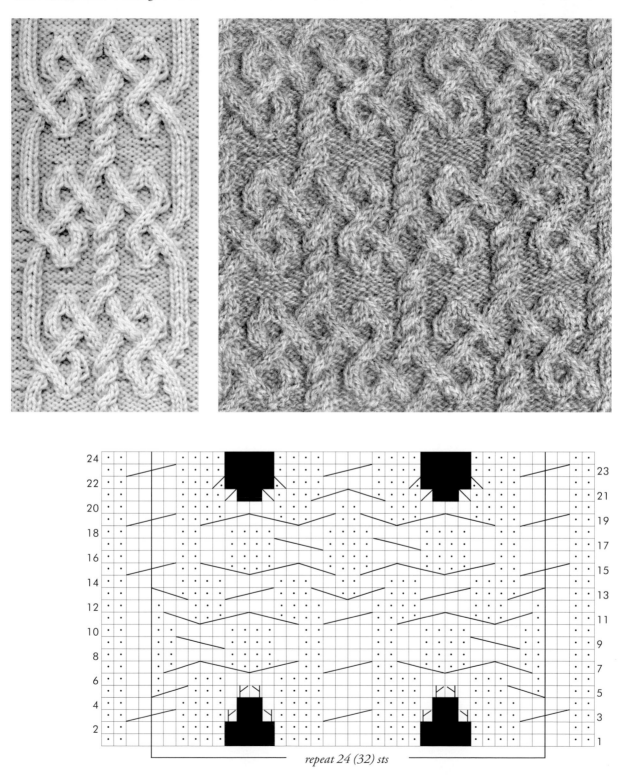

repeat 24 (32) sts

FJALAR
Sweater and hat

In this neat little sweater, I've put the pattern in the ribbing by alternating flipped bands of angular S-hitches from Ardre with plain ribbing. The collar is a panel of the same pattern overlapped at the front, and the same pattern appears in the warm and becoming hat. That the hat in this color is reminiscent of a chanterelle is an extra fillip.

Sizes: S (M) L

Finished measurements: Bust 38½/98 (41¾/106) 44¾/114 in/cm. Waist, 26¾/68 (30¾/78) 33/84 in/cm. Length, 20¾/53 (21¼/55) 21¼/57 in/cm. Head measurement for hat, 21½-22¾ in/55-58 cm.

Materials: 10 (11) 12 balls Fjord + 3 balls for hat.

Needles: 3 mm and 4 mm needles and 40 cm long 3 mm and 4 mm circular needles for cap.

Tension: 22 sts x 30 rows in stockinette on 4 mm needles = 4 inches square or 10 x 10 cm. 36 st pattern = 5 inches/13 cm. Watch your tension carefully, and adjust needle size accordingly.

Back

With 3 mm needles, cast on 98 (110) 118 sts and k chart on p. 84. First row is on wrong side of work. **Note:** Before starting pattern: **Size S:** k 1 selvage st, (k 2, p 2) 3 times, k 2 widthwise repeats of charted pattern starting at row 0 (= 72 pattern sts), (k 2 p 2) 3 times, k 1 selvage st. **Size M:** k 1 selvage st, k across row 0 of chart three times (108 sts), k 1 selvage st. **Size L:** K 1 selvage st, k 2 p 2, k across row 0 of chart 3 times (108 sts), k 2 p 2, k 1 selvage st. K 5 rows in same pattern, then continue chart, for 2 vertical pattern repeats. Change to 4 mm circular needle and stockinette st. Inc 1 st each side every 12th row 7 times = 112 (124) 132 sts. When work measures 20/51 (20½/53) 21½/55 in/cm, bind off at shoulder edge at beginning of every row: 9,9,9,9 (8, 9, 8, 9, 8) 7, 8, 8, 8, 8, 7 sts (Bind off each number on both sides). Then bind off the remaining 40 center sts.

Front

Knit like back until work measures 12½/32 (13¼/34) 14/36 in/cm. Mark the center 24 sts for the collar, put the sts for the left side on a holder and k the right side. Cast on a new selvage st at the neck edge (on the right side) k selvage st, k 3, p 2, k 2, k 16 sts of pattern panel, k 2, p 2, and k stockinette to end of row. Continuing, k into k sts, p into p, except for the 16 pattern sts. K these following the chart. On the next row, the base of the collar is formed with short rows (while repeating rows 1 + 2 on chart): K 10 sts, yarn over, turn and k back. K 20 sts (knit the yarn over with the st following it), yarn over, turn and k back. K 10 sts, yarn over, turn and knit back. After this, k straight up. When collar measures 8 cm, k 2 sts together just inside the 30 stockinette sts of the shoulder. Dec like this every 6th row altogether 6 times. When front is as long as back, bind off on shoulder side 9, 9, 9, 9 sts (8, 9, 8, 9, 8 sts) 7, 8, 8, 8, 8, 7 sts at beginning of every 2nd row. Cast on a new selvage st on the shoulder side of the neckband, and continue on these 30 sts, until it reaches the center back of the neck. Bind off. *Left side:* Pick up sts from holder and cast on 29 new sts on the neck edge. K like the right front except: K chart for left side on p. 84 (Begin short rows on the wrong side of the work and k 2 sts farther before turning.), and dec using SSK.

Sleeves

With 3 mm needles, cast on 46 (54) 62 sts and k pattern immediately. The first row is on the wrong side of work. Set up pattern before you begin the chart: (K 2, p 2) 1 (2) 3 times, k Row 0 of chart (38 sts), then (p 2, k 2) 1 (2) 3 times. K Row 0 five times, then Rows 1-26. After completing 1 vertical repeat, inc 1 st each side every 4th row altogether 7 times (= 60 (68) 76 sts). K the new sts in ribbing. After 2 vertical repeats, change to 4 mm needles and stockinette st. Inc 1 st each side every 4th row 20 times (= 100 (108) 116 sts). When sleeve measures 18/46 (17¾/45) 17¼/44 in/cm, bind off 6 sts at beginning of every row 16 times. Bind off. K an identical sleeve.

Assembly

Block all pieces. Sew shoulder seams. Sew backs of collar together and tack to back of neck. Tack base of left side of neck band front invisibly inside right neck band front. Sew in sleeves, matching center top to shoulder seam and allowing 8½/22 (9½/24) 10¼/26 in/cm front and back for armhole. Sew underarm and side seams continuously.

Hat

With 3 mm circular needle, cast on 119 sts and k around in k 2, p 2 ribbing for 3 in/8 cm. Change to 4 mm circular needle and k a dec round as follows: *k 1, p 2, SSK, p 6, k 2 together, k 1, p 2, k 1.* Repeat * - * (Row 1 on chart) 7 times, knitting the last 2 sts of rnd together = 105 sts. K Row 1 of chart for 8 rnds, k into k, p into p. Now k Rows 1-16 and begin to inc (make 1) between each right and left panel, that is, on the central rib between each 2 panels. Make a right inc before the ribbing and a left inc after the rib (= 12 inc sts per rnd.) *Inc every other rnd twice, then k 2 rnds without increasing. Repeat from * four times = 201 sts. K Rows 1 and 2 again to finish. Then k 1 rnd and p 3 rnds (the edge of the crown). *Crown*: K in stockinette. Divide work into 6 parts, alternately 34 and 33 sts each. Dec by SSK at the beginning and by k 2 together at the end of every section every other rnd until 12 sts remain. K 2 sts together around, break yarn and pull tail through remaining sts. Work tail into wrong side.

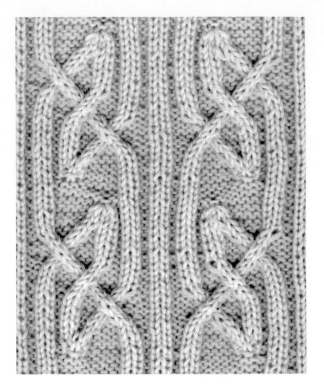

The S-Hitch can also be knitted in an angular version. Above: Pattern swatch with left and right facing s-hitches knitted using the chart below, the same used for Fjalar. Row 0 is for Fjalar only. Rows 1 and 2 can be knitted once or repeated indefinitely.

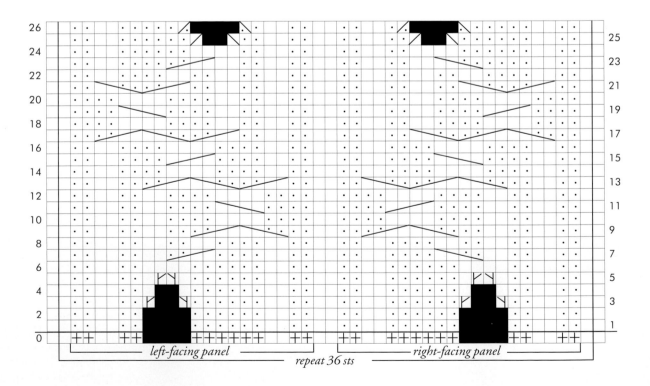

left-facing panel

right-facing panel

repeat 36 sts

FREYA

Blouse with Vendel figure-eight knots

Freya is the name I gave this little, feminine sweater blouse, shaped with a light hand and accented along the front edges with the smart figure-eight knot panel from Vendel.

Sizes: XS (S) M (L) XL
Finished measurements: Bust, 35½/90 (37¾/96) 39¼/100 (41¾/106) 44/112 in/cm. Length, 23½/60 (23½/60) 25¼/64 (25¼/64) 25¼/64 in/cm.
Materials: 5 (6) 7 (8) 9 skeins Silketweed. 5 small buttons. (Alternate yarn: 6 (7) 7 (8) 9 - 50 g skeins Soft Woolsilk.)
Needles: 2.5 mm and 3 mm.
Tension: 24 sts x 34 rows in stockinette on 3 mm needles = 4 inches square or 10 x 10 cm. The 16 sts x 32 rows of the pattern panel = 2 x 3¾ in/5 x 9.5 cm. Watch your tension closely and adjust your needle size accordingly.
Pattern: Follow the chart for *Vendel, right and left*. The larger sizes become longer by knitting Rows 1 and 2 an additional time between knot motifs.

Back

With 2.5 mm needles, cast on 108 (116) 120 (128) 134 sts and k 5 rows (garter st). The first row is on the wrong side of work. Change to 3 mm needles and stockinette. Dec 1 st each side every 8th row 5 (6) 6 (7) 8 times = 98 (104) 108 (114) 118 sts. When work measures 9¾/25 (9½/24) 10½/27 (10¼/26) 9¾/25 in/cm, inc 1 st each side every 10th (10th) 8th (8th) 6th row 5 (6) 6 (7) 8 times = 108 (116) 120 (128) 134 sts. When work measures 15¾/40 (15¼/39) 16½/42 (16/41) 15½/40 in/cm, bind off for armhole beginning of every row 4, 3 (4, 4) 4, 4 (5, 4, 2) 5, 5, 2 sts (Use every number once on each side.), then 1 st both sides every 2nd row 2 (4) 5 (5) 6 times = 90 (92) 94 (96) 98 sts. When armhole measures 7½/19 (7¾/20) 8¼/21 (8½/22) 9/23 in/cm, bind off for shoulders at beginning of next 6 rows: 9, 9, 10 (9, 10, 10) 9, 10, 10 (10, 10, 10) 10, 10, 11 sts. Bind off the remaining 34 (34) 36 (36) 36 center sts.

Left front

With 2.5 mm needles, cast on 58 (62) 64 (68) 71 sts and set up the pattern on the first row (on wrong side): k selvage st, p 2, 16 sts following Row 0 of chart for *left panel* (p. 87), p 2, then k the rest of the sts (garter st). K this row back and forth for 5 rows. Change to 3 mm needles and follow *left panel* chart Rows 1-32 for panel with remaining

of the sts in stockinette. Dec and inc following the plan for the back on the sleeve side. When work measures 15¾/40 (15¾/39) 16½/42 (16/41) 15¾/40 in/cm, bind off for armhole as on back. After the 5th repeat of the entire pattern panel, and when work measures about 49 (49) 53 (53) 53 cm, put 11 sts on a holder for the neck and bind off (on the neck side) every 2nd row first 4, 2 (4, 2) 4, 3 (4, 3) 4, 3 sts, then 2, 1, 1 sts in all sizes. When armhole measures 7½/19 (7¾/20) 8¼/21 (8½/22) 9/23 in/cm, bind off for shoulder 9, 9, 10 (9, 10, 10) 9, 10, 10 (10, 10, 10) 10, 10, 11 sts.

Right front

K mirror image to left front, using *right panel* chart for the pattern panel.

Sleeves

On 2.5 mm needles, cast on 44 (46) 48 (50) 52 sts and k 5 rows (garter st). Change to 3 mm needles and stockinette st. After 10 rows, inc 1 st each side every 6th row 19 (20) 20 (21) 22 times = 82 (86) 88 (92) 96 sts. When sleeve is 16½/42 (16½/42) 17/43 (17¼/44) 17¼/44 in/cm long, bind off for sleeve cap: 4, 3 (4, 4) 4, 4 (5, 4) 5, 5 sts on each side. Then, dec 1 st every 2nd row until 26 sts remain. Bind off 2 sts beginning of every row 6 times (3 times each side). Bind off last 14 sts.

Assembly

Block all pieces. *Left front band:* With 2.5 mm needles, pick up 127 (127) 135 (135) 135 sts and k 4 rows (garter st). Bind off in knitting on wrong side of work. Mark positions of 5 buttons, the highest ½ in/1 cm from the top, the lowest about 11/28 (11/28) 12½/31 (12½/31) 12¼/31 in/cm from the top, and the others distributed evenly in between. *Right front band:* Pick up sts and k front band as on left front, but on Row 2, k buttonholes opposite button markings. For each buttonhole, bind off 2 sts and cast on 2 sts above holes, in the next row. K rest of front band as on left front. Sew shoulder seams. *Collar:* With 2.5 mm needles, pick up 122 (122) 126 (126) 126 sts around the neck inside the front bands. K garter st and

shape collar with short rows: K 4 sts, yo, turn and k back. K 4 sts farther (knitting yo with the st following it), yarn over, turn, and k back. In this way k 4 sts farther each row until you have turned 10 times. K to other end of collar and form the point in the same way. Now k across the whole row and inc: 1 st 4 sts from the edge every 6th row (right inc at beginning of row, left inc at end of row), and 1 st every 6th row at shoulder seams. When collar measures a good 6 cm at center back, bind off all sts in k from the underside of collar. Sew underarm seams. Sew side seams. Sew sleeves into armholes. Sew on buttons.

Vendel Figure-eight knots, like the S-hitch from Ardre has two strands. While one strand whips diagonally from side to side, the second is thrown around it and itself in an intricate figure-eight knot. Rows 1-2 can be repeated to change the distance between knots. Freja and the pattern swatch are knitted following the charts below. Row 0 is for Freja only.

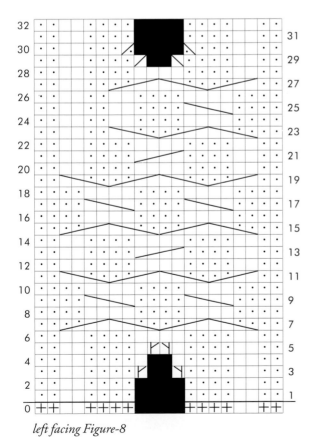

Both the S-hitch from Ardre in its most basic form and Vendel Figure-Eights decorate the end plate of a Skåne drinking horn (left).

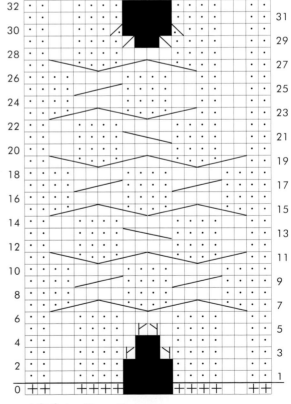

left facing Figure-8

right facing Figure-8

The Lillbjärs border

A handsome and intricate border of interlinked half-hitches frames this picture stone from Lillbjärs in Stenkyrka parish on Gotland and other Gotland picture stones. It also edges a number of buckles and a buckler from Valsgärde.

Go with me on a journey in pattern analysis around the edge of the picture stone at right, and compare with the diagram on the next page: The border design is made up of three knotted strands, in which the first strand makes a half-hitch around the diagonal of the second strand, passes the second strand's half-hitch, and finally becomes the diagonal around which a half-hitch in the third strand is knotted. All three strands repeat this exactly.

The border was difficult to translate into knitting. If you follow the same system as for earlier patterns, the decreases from one motif would flow into the increases for the next, and look completely off.

To knit the pattern at all, one has to place the paired increases one row later than in the other patterns. Thus, they're worked on the wrong side. The decreases, in turn, must be one row earlier that usual, so that the first dec is worked on the wrong side and the second on the following row on the right side. This makes the border more difficult to knit, but it is so good looking that it should be worth the trouble. As usual, a mirrored version is also given in the charts.

The marvelous picture stone from Lillbjärs on Gotland (Sweden).

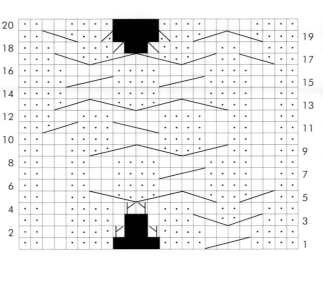

Chart and pattern swatches show the Lillbjärs border the "right" way and flipped mirror image.

Pattern analysis sketch, above left.

Illustration: The Lillbjärs border edges a little decorative concho from Valsgärde, Uppland, Sweden.

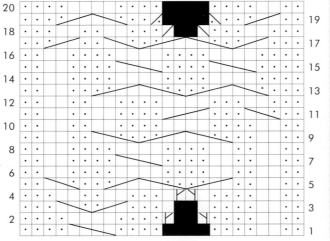

The pattern appears on the nosepiece of the magnificent Viking era helmet found in Coppergate, York, England, braided into two mirrored borders. The same pattern is found on the side of a box clasp from Klinte, Gotland, Sweden, a good example of how the same pattern can be expressed for different purposes in different places. Itself reason enough to visit the museum in York, this gorgeous helmet is also emblematic of the desire to beautify everyday things — a desire that you and I find an outlet for in knitting.

During my analysis of this pattern, I found that by putting an extra crossover between repeats in the braided version, the increases and decreases can be spaced as usual, considerably simplifying the knitting of the border.

Facing page: The gorgeous helmet from York, England

This page:
Box clasp from Klinte, Gotland

Pattern swatch and chart for the braided Lillbjärs border

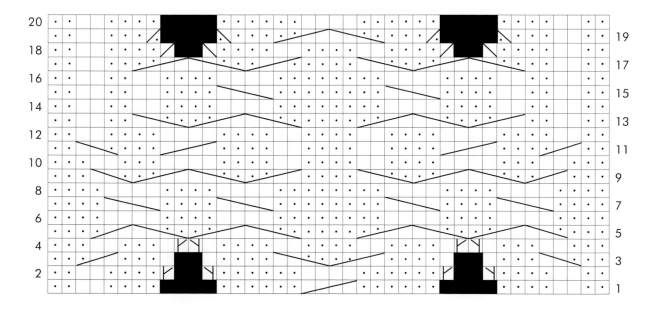

Runes

The oral tradition was pre-eminent for the Vikings, and skalds and storytellers were highly revered, but finds in our own times have shown that the Vikings also wrote, and in much greater volume than had been assumed earlier.

Starting in the first century of the Christian era, Nordic peoples used runes. At the beginning of the Viking period, an alphabet of runes containing sixteen signs was in use. It was called "futhark," the word created by reading the first six signs in order.

Runic writing probably developed through encounters with Latin letters, from which a number of signs were adopted, without laying much weight on their Latin phonetic values.

Runes are designed to be cut into wood and consist of vertical and diagonal lines which were cut across the grain. Horizontal lines, which risked splitting the wood and would have been hard to see and cut, were not used.

Runes were used to write all kinds of texts, but because of the nature of in-scription, the messages tended to be short. Runic inscriptions on stones can be, for example, monuments for people who have died, often in foreign countries. On some stones property or inheritance is proclaimed, as on the somewhat boastful stones at Jarlabanke's Bridge in Täby, Uppland, where Jarlabanke let it be known that he owned all of Täby. A little wooden marking tag states, "Sigmund owns this bag."

On a rune stone at Vallentuna church, Uppland, Jarlabanke, the top kick in Täby a thousand years ago, proclaims among other things that "he alone owns the whole hundred."

On a rune staff from Sigtuna (Sweden) two different people have inscribed flattering observations about the king: "The king is the most hospitable. He gave the most. He is well liked."

And on another, newly found rune staff, also from Sigtuna, as many as ninety-three runes were cut. The text has not been completely interpreted at the time of this writing, but it seems to be a spell against sickness. The last words are, ". . . fly away fever."

There are also examples of ordinary graffiti, the same kind one sees today, where the writer was saying, "I was here. I exist," by inscribing his name. A loop of runes on the shoulder of the lion at Pireus in Greece is unfortu-nately so deteriorated that its meaning is lost to us.

In the futhark on the facing page are all sixteen runic letters in the Danish, or common, runic alphabet with their phonetic values.

ᚠᚢᚦᚨᚱᚲ ᚺᚾᛁᛏᛋ ᛏᛒᛘᛚᛦ

f	u	th	o	r	k		h	n	i	a	s		t	b	m	l	R
v	v		a		g		g		e	ä			d	p			e
o			ä		nk				ä	e			nt				
ü			ng						ä	ü			nd				
ö										y							

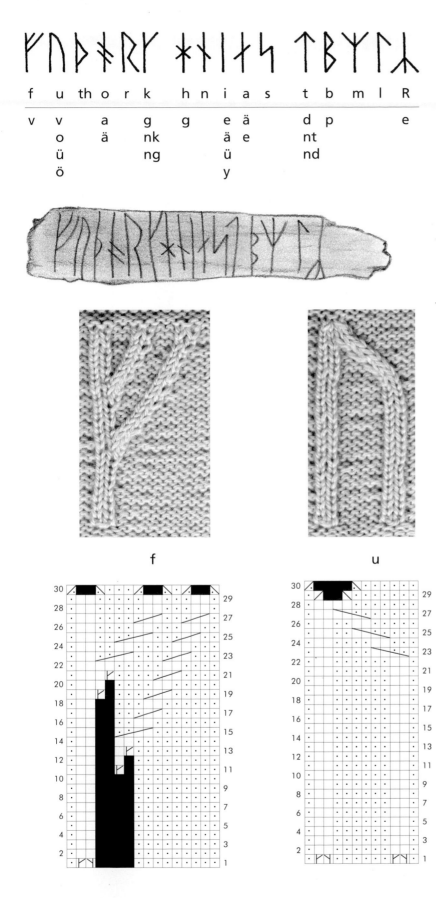

I was excited to see that the basic assumptions for knitting runes in relief were much like those for inscribing them in wood—that is, vertical and diagonal lines were easy and horizontal lines didn't work at all.

On this and following pages, you will find all the common runes translated to knitting with accompanying charts.

The complete futhark with alternative phonetic values, and an early example of the academic tradition in Lund, today a Swedish university town—a bit of bone inscribed with the whole futhark.

f

u

th

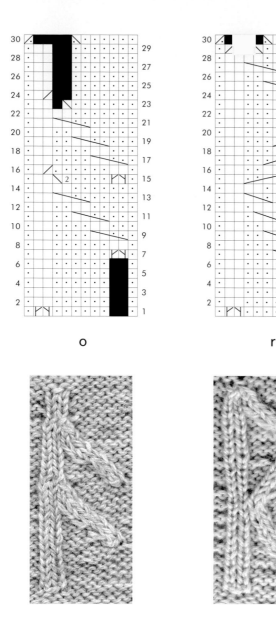

o

r

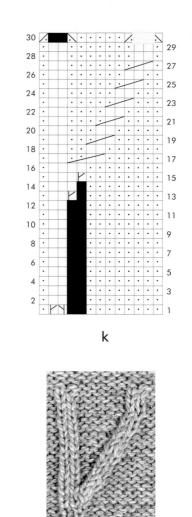

k

You should be aware of some technical points when knitting your own passages in runes.

The space between letters affects the visual rhythm of words and must be adjusted here and there. Although the runes are designed to be knitted with two stitch spaces, if two uprights wind up next to each other, as the *i* and the *k* do in the word *kysmik*, a couple of extra stitches are needed so they don't pull into each other like ribbing.

In other cases the space between signs becomes rather too large, as between *s* and *m* in *kysmik*, and one has to place the signs closer together, in this case laying out the charts so they overlap slightly. For example, a little of the *m* lies inside the chart space of the *s*. (See chart on p. 98.)

The space between words is effectively marked with punctuation —a little square, an *x,* or a dot. The chart for a dot is at right.

Diagram for dot

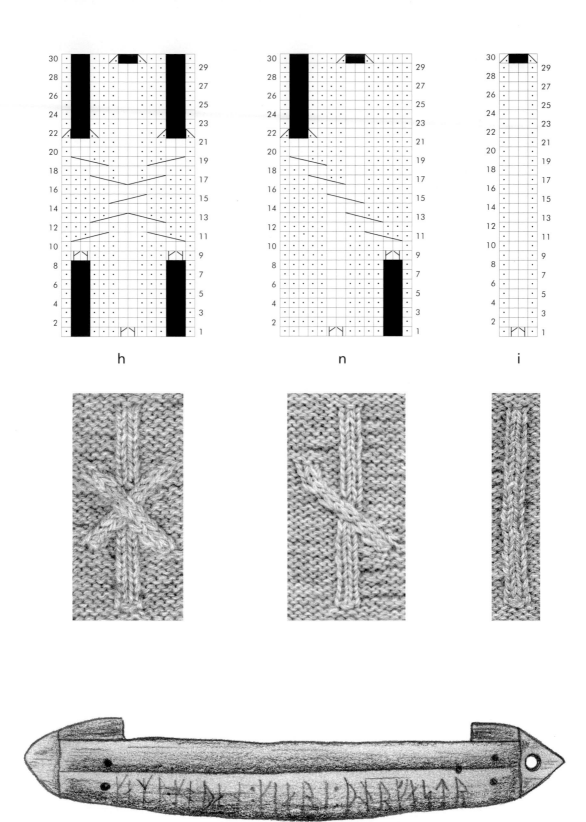

h   n   i

Bone comb handle from Lincoln, England. The inscription reads, "Thorfast made a good comb."

KYSMIK
Vest and child's pullover with runes

On a bit of bone from Norway, a love smitten young man inscribed "Kysmik" —kiss me. The vest decorated with this hopeful device is classic in shape to be worn by either gender. On the child's sweater, the same invitation is repeated with a pagan happiness symbol—St. John's cross—underneath. The sweater fits loosely and the Soft Woolsilk isn't scratchy.

Vest

Sizes: Unisex S (M) L (XL)

Finished measurements: Chest, 42½/108 (44/112) 47¼/ 120 (48¾/124) in/cm. Length, 24/61 (24¾/63) 25½/65 (26¼/67) in/cm.

Materials: 4 (4) 5 (5) skeins Yllets Ullgarn 3.

Needles: 3.5 mm and 4 mm needles. 3.5 mm circular needle for neck ribbing.

Tension: 20 sts x 26 rows in stockinette on 4 mm needles = 4 inches square or 10 x 10 cm. Check your tension with a swatch in stockinette and while knitting the sweater.

Back

With 3.5 mm needles, cast on 110 (114) 122 (126) sts and p 2, k 2 ribbing for 3 in/8 cm. (The first row is on the wrong side.) Be sure you have 2 k sts on both edges on the right side. Change to 4 mm needles and knit reverse stockinette. When work measures 13¼/37 (15/38) 15¼/ 39 (15¾/40) in/cm, bind off for armhole 4, 3, 2 (4, 3, 2) 5, 3, 2 (5, 3, 2) sts, (using every number on both edges once). Then dec 1 st each side every second row 5 (5) 6 (6) times = 82 (86) 90 (94) sts. When armhole measures 8½/ 22 (9/23) 9½/24 (9¾/25) in/cm, place the center 30 (30) 32 (32) sts on a holder and k each side separately. Bind off an additional 3 sts on the neck side while binding off shoulders: 11, 12 (12, 13) 13, 13 (14, 14) sts.

Front

K like the back, but when work measures 30 (31) 32 (33) sts, k runes on the center 52 sts, following chart on p. 98 (or your own variation). After the armhole decs, divide work at center for V-neck and knit each side separately. Bind off on the neck side 1 st every second row 18 (18) 19 (19) times. Dec for shoulder at the same height and in the same way as on the back.

Assembly

Block both pieces. Sew shoulder seams. ***V-neck:*** With 3.5 mm circular needle, pick up 144 (148) 152 (156) sts around the neck. K 2, p 2 ribbing, beginning and ending the row with a selvage st and 2 k sts on the right side. (You are knitting back and forth, *flat.*) Rib for 3 cm, and bind off in ribbing. Tack short edges of band to opposite sides of v-neck. ***Armhole edging:*** In the same way, pick up 106 (110) 114 (118) sts around arm hole, rib— k 2, p 2—for 1 in/3 cm and bind off in ribbing. Repeat on other armhole. Sew side seams.

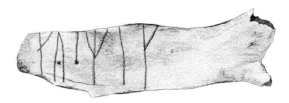

Child's pullover

Sizes: 2 (4) 6 (8) years.

Finished measurements: Chest, 28¼/72 (30/76) 31½/80 (33/84) in/cm. Length, 15/38 (15¾/40) 16½/42 (17½/ 45) in/cm.

Materials: 3 (4) 4 (5) skeins of Soft Woolsilk.

Needles: 2.5 mm and 3 mm. 2.5 mm circular needle.

Tension: 23 sts x 34 rows in stockinette on 3 mm needles = 10 x 10 cm. Check your tension with a swatch in stockinette before beginning and check while knitting project.

Pattern: Knit the happiness sign following chart on p. 30, "kysmik" following chart on p. 98.

Front

With 2.5 mm needles, cast on 86 (90) 94 (98) sts and rib, p 2, k 2, for 1½/4 (1½/4) 2/5 (2/5) in/cm. The first row is on wrong side of sweater, but each row should start and finish with k 2 on front side of work. Change to 3 mm needles and k reverse stockinette. When work measures 4/10 (4¼/11) 4¾/12 (5½/14) in/cm, k a *little happiness sign* in center, following chart on p. 30. At 7¾/20 (8¼/21) 9/23 (9¾/25) in/cm, k runic inscription on center 52 sts — 17 (19) 21 (23) sts from edges. When work measures 12½/32 (13¼/34) 14¼/36 (15/38) in/cm, put center 24 (24) 26 (26) sts on a holder and k each side separately. On neck side, dec 1 st every second row 5 times. When work measures 15¾/40 (16½/42) 16½/42 (17½/45) in/cm, bind off shoulders.

Back

Knit like front but with no patterning. The neckline begins only when work measures 14¼/36 (15/38) 15¾/40 (17/43) in/cm. Then put center 30 (30) 32 (32) sts on a holder and k each side separately. Dec 1 st on neck edge every second row twice. Bind off shoulders at same height as front.

Sleeves

With 2.5 mm needles, cast on 42 (42) 46 (46) sts and rib, p 2, k 2 for 2 in/5 cm. The first row will be on the wrong side, but *right side of work* starts and ends with 2 k sts, so start with p 2. Change to 3 mm needles and reverse stockinette. Inc both sides every 4th row 16 (18) 18 (21) times = 74 (78) 82 (88) sts. When sleeve measures 9¾/25 (11/28) 12½/32 (13¾/35) in/cm, bind off. K another identical sleeve.

Assembly

Block all pieces to measure between damp towels and let the whole pile dry. Sew the shoulder seams. *Neck edge:* With 2.5 mm circular needle, pick up 90 (90) 94 (94) sts around the neck and rib k 2, p 2 for 1 in/2.5 cm. Bind off in ribbing. Sew sleeves in, matching shoulder seam to center point of sleeve top and allowing 6¼/16 (6½/17) 7/18 (7½/19) in/cm front and back for the sleeve. Sew side. and underarm sleeves continuously.

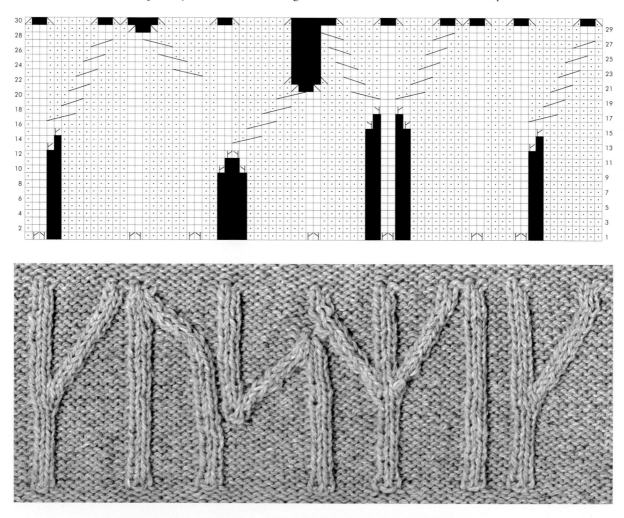

If you look more closely at the runes on the rune bone with the old Nordic inscription "kysmik" (kiss me), you will see that the signs do not precisely correspond to the common runes of the futhark.

Common runes didn't encompass all the different sounds found in the spoken language and so in the end of the Viking era, "dotted runes" appeared, which used an additional dot on some letters to change the phonetic value. In this way, *u* could be changed to *ü;* the *i* rune, to *e;* the *t* rune, to *d;* the *k* rune, hard *g;* and the *b* rune, to *p.*

The *S* on the bone is cut as a *kortkvist* rune—a "short-twigged" rune. Kortkvist runes are a parallel runic system, where the signs are simplified by further shortening the short diagonals and replacing some signs. The *s,* for example, has become a single short line in the upper half of the space.

The rune bone from Sigtuna, Sweden, the one maintaining that the king is best, is inscribed with *kortkvist* runes.

Rune inscribing is strenuous, testing patience, especially if the runes are to be inscribed in stone, so it's hardly surprising that inscribers took shortcuts when they could. Even the 16-letter futhark presented here in knitting is a simplification of an earlier runic system with twenty-four letters.

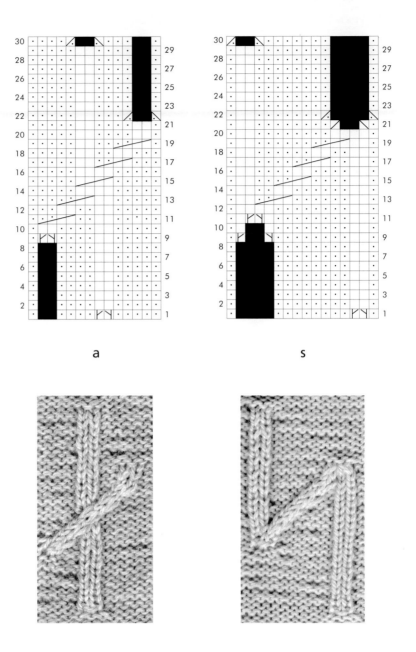

a   s

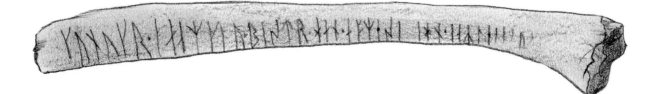

Royal rune bone, found in Sigtuna, Uppland, Sweden

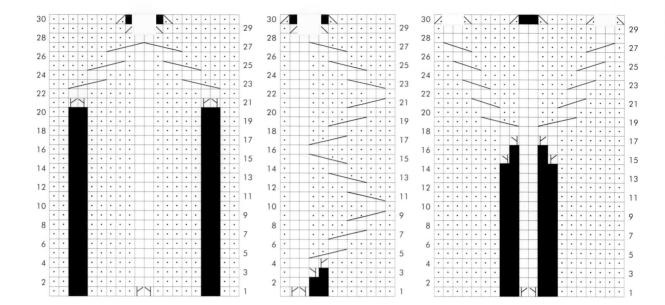

t

b

m

Marker block from Trondheim, Norway

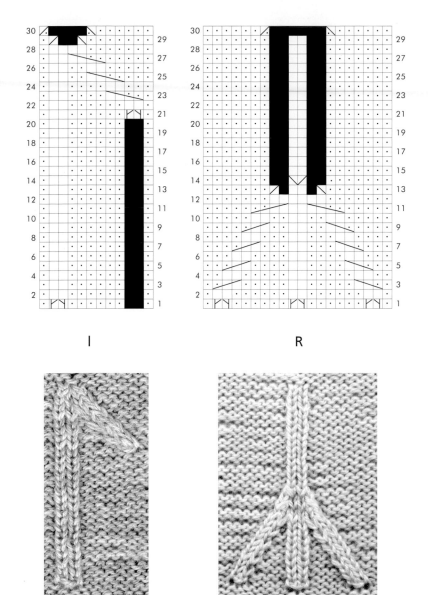

I

R

Notice that the rune written with an upper case "R" is not an ordinary "r" sound but expresses the "rs" sound at the end of a word, as in "force."

It's also worth pointing out that the phonetic information here, the correspondance to Latin letters, is not exact. This is problematic for today's runologists and for you, should you want to transcribe your name or a text to runes.

If you're not so fortunate as to have an Old Nordic name already found in rune transcription, the best thing to do, if possible, is to consult with someone who knows runes.

But don't worry. Even Vikings made spelling errors.

Calendar staff from Nyköping, Södermanland

Intertwined Creatures

Twisted and knotted animals were fundamental to the Nordic ornamental idiom in the Iron Age and the Viking era.

These are often creatures distorted into long bands—dragons and snakes—but other and less clearly identifiable four-footed animals appear, as well as a number of birds.

The clasp from Tróllaskógur, Iceland, clearly shows a deer wound about with snakes, but who but an expert can see that it is an animal twined around itself on the bone needle from Trondheim?

In the decoration on a Gotland box clasp, it almost seems that a birdlike creature is bound by a ring in a motif much like the quartered ring pattern on p. 15.

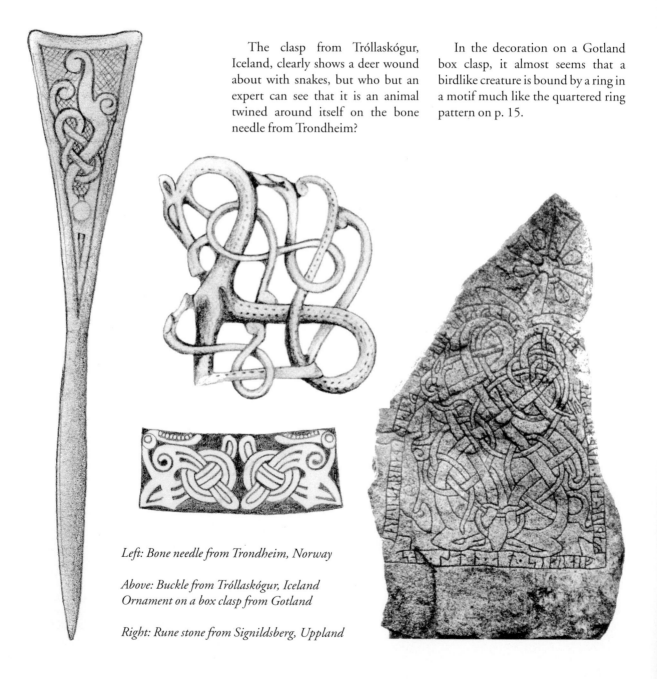

Left: Bone needle from Trondheim, Norway

*Above: Buckle from Tróllaskógur, Iceland
Ornament on a box clasp from Gotland*

Right: Rune stone from Signildsberg, Uppland

On the rune stone from Signilds-berg, Upplands-Bro, Sweden, two rune animals intertwine with each other and what seems to be snakes in a complicated pattern.

The simple rune animal cut into a traveling tablet in Upplands Väsby (right) has an elegant head and neck crest. The tail is flung in a loop around its neck in a hitch like that in the Lillbjärs border.

On the little bronze plate from Norway (lower right) the animal lies in an "S." We might recognize the *S-hitch from Ardre*, but again, it could be read as two loops of the simpler version of the curly zigzag (p. 34).

The little snake (below), a decoration on a beam that was once part of a stave church in Hørning, Denmark, has twined itself into the figure-eight knot (p. 70).

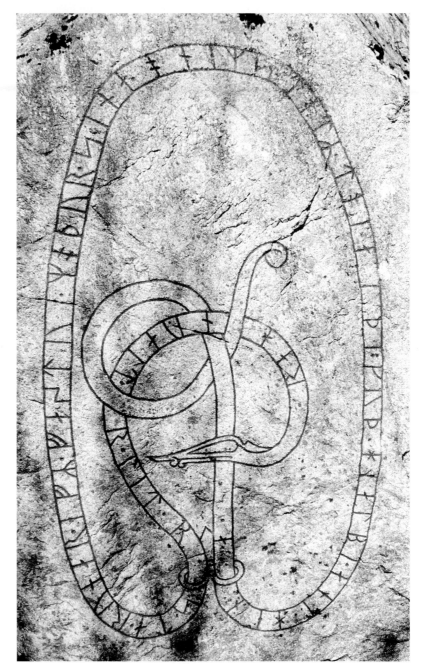

Left, above: Decoration on a plank, from Hørning, Denmark
Right, above: Rune slab, from Ed, Upplands Väsby, Uppland, Sweden.
Lower right: Gilded bronze plate from Hedemarken, Norway.

Fafner

Intertwined rune animal cushion with mat knot border

In Fafner—a dwarf who was changed into a dragon—I have combined pretty much all the techniques presented in the book. I put a dragon-like animal in the center, but another motif, like a happiness sign or a large mat knot (p. 44) would also be handsome. Or, you could cover it with the allover version of Bjärs hitches (p. 28).

Finished measurements: About 15¾/40 x 15¾/40 in/cm.
Materials: 200 g of U84
Needles: 4 mm.
Tension: 20 sts in stockinette on 4 mm needles = 4 inches or 10 cm. Check your tension by knitting a swatch before you start the project.
Pattern: Knitted following chart on p. 106 and p. 109.

Center panel

Cast on 50 sts and k reverse stockinette for 1¼ in/3 cm. Next 28 rows: p 18 sts, then follow chart on p 106 for 26 sts, and end with 18 sts. On Row 29, put the 4 sts marked * on a holder in front of the work, then cast on 2 new sts behind them. Continue in reverse stockinette until work measures 9¾ in/25cm. Bind off. Put the 4 sts from the holder on a needle and knit the left facing dragon head.

Framing

Cast on 28 sts. *K lattice pattern Rows 1-8 for about 9¾ in/25 cm (the length of a side on the center panel), then k corner following charts (pp. 108-109). Repeat from * 3 more times until you have 4 corners.

Assembly

Block pieces to measure, lay a damp cloth over them and let the whole pile dry completely. Pin dragon's head to shape in place and tack down with a few small, invisible stitches (See p. 106). Graft the 2 mitered ends together. Sew the center panel to the framing the same way. Cut a back from fabric, leaving about ½ in/1.5 cm seam allowance. Press/fabric seam allowances in, then overcast the front and back together inside the selvage sts.

Left-facing dragon head

Put the 4 sts from the holder on a needle and cast on a selvage st on each side. Start on the right side, and p all wrong-side rows. **Rows 1, 3, 5:** K 6. **Row 7:** K 3, turn. **Row 8:** P. **Row 9:** K 1, inc 1, k 5 = 7 sts. **Row 11:** Inc 1 st in the second st of the row = 8 sts. **Row 13:** Inc 1 sts in the second st of the row = 9 sts. **Row 15:** K 2 together, k 5, SSK = 7 sts. **Row 17:** K 3, yarn over, k 3. **Row 18:** P 4, slip the yarnover and make a yarnover, p 3. **Row 19:** K 2, slip the next st, k the 2 yarnovers together and pass the slipped st over, k 4. **Row 21:** K 2, double SSK, k 2. **Row 23:** K 2, SSK, k 1. **Row 25:** K 4. **Row 26:** P the first 2 sts together and bind off.

Right-facing dragon head

Pick up 4 sts from holder, cast on a selvage st at both edges. Start on the right side and p all even rows.
Rows 1, 3, 5: K 6. **Row 6:** P 3. **Row 7:** Turn and k back. **Row 9:** Inc 1 st in the next to last st = 7 sts. **Row 11:** Inc 1 st in the next to last st = 8 sts. **Row 13:** Inc 1 st in the next to last st = 9 sts. **Row 15:** K 2 together, k 5, SSK. **Row 17:** K 4, yarn over, k 3. **Row 18:** P 3, slip yarnover, make a yarn over, p 4. **Row 19:** K 4, k the 2 yarnovers together with the next st. k 2. **Row 21:** K 2, k 3 together, k 2. **Row 23:** K 1, k 2 together, k 2. **Row 25:** K 4. **Row 27:** K first 2 sts together and bind off.

The afghan is made by sewing together many pattern swatches knitted for the book.

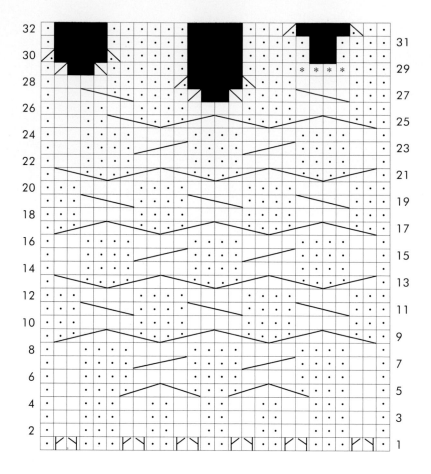

Above: Chart for Fafner

Below: Pattern swatches showing left and right facing dragon heads (left) and an example of embroidered details on a dragon head (right).

For chart and directions for knitting around the corner, turn the page.

As you can see, plaiting techniques are also built into the intertwined animals, however usually a little more free-form. To knit them, you will also have to use somewhat free-er techniques.

The dragon head is knitted on a single cable with a 4-stitch strand, on a loose 4-st cable, or, as in Fafner, by extending the point of the lattice pattern.

Basically, you put 4 (k) sts on a holder where you want the head to be, cast on 2 sts behind these, and finish the background in reverse stockinette. (The background at this point requires fewer sts, because there are no more cable crosses to pull it up.) When the background is finished, pick up the sts from the holder and k the head following the directions.

Then you will shape the head and tack it down to the background. To do this, you use appliqué techniques that can be used for entire animals and allow you much freedom in shaping the motif. The motif can be finished off with embroidered details as shown in the example below.

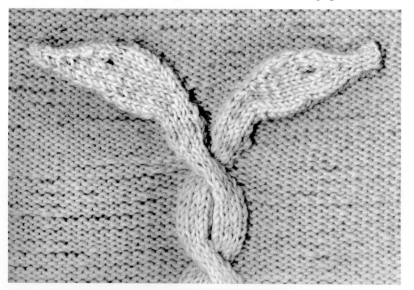

The fantastic metal plate from Mandal, Norway, is a sampler of at least six of the patterns in this book. There are also exciting interlacings of rune animals.

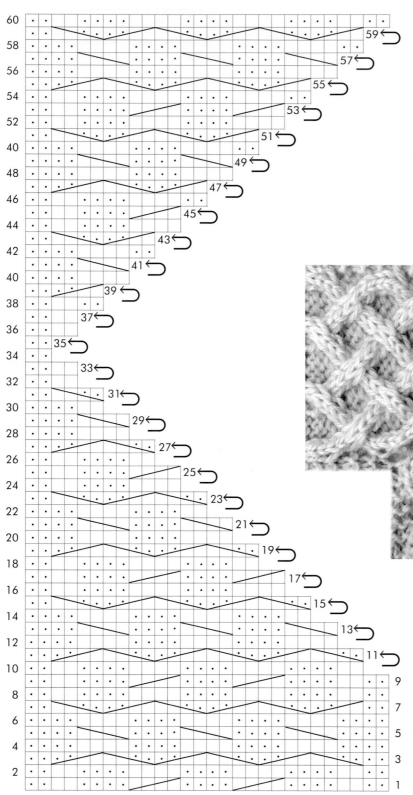

Knitting around corners

Sometime while I was working with all these plaited patterns, I got the idea of knitting corners as a border on a pillow or a jacket. The Irish game board on p. 42 was one of the artifacts that moved my thoughts in that direction. What I wanted to achieve was naturally to have the bands in the pattern continue without a break, plaited over and under one another at a right angle.

Chart on this page shows a right corner (that is, a corner that turns right). A corresponding left corner is shown on the facing page.

The patterns swatch above shows a left (turning) corner.

The logical technique to use, described in detail in the next section, is knitted short rows. However, the first short row turning method, of wrapping the yarn around the st after the turning point, disturbed the pattern structure. The second method, using a yarnover, didn't work either, because there are crossed stitches where the short row rejoins and the yarnover is in the way.

After much experimentation and many test swatches, what I came up with was to make short rows with, simply, a plain turn. The holes that of course happen, almost entirely disappear under the crosses of the plaiting and are not obvious. The rows are knitted successively shorter and then longer.

If you want a more open angle, or a completely rounded border, make the short rows shorter and the distance between them greater. The angle of the corner (or the shape of the curve) along with the appearance of the plaiting are the critical factors here. Chart this, drawing 5-6 repeats and marking what you think needs to be eliminated. Knit a test swatch and based on it, correct your chart. Knit a new test swatch. . .

The chart on these two pages is a corner in the pattern *Wide lattice plaiting*. The diagram shows both left and right corners, but you will use only the left corner in Fafner, the cushion.

You will encounter the right corner in the pattern *Zigzag overhand knots* on Vebjörg, where it's used on the shoulder to corner the yoke.

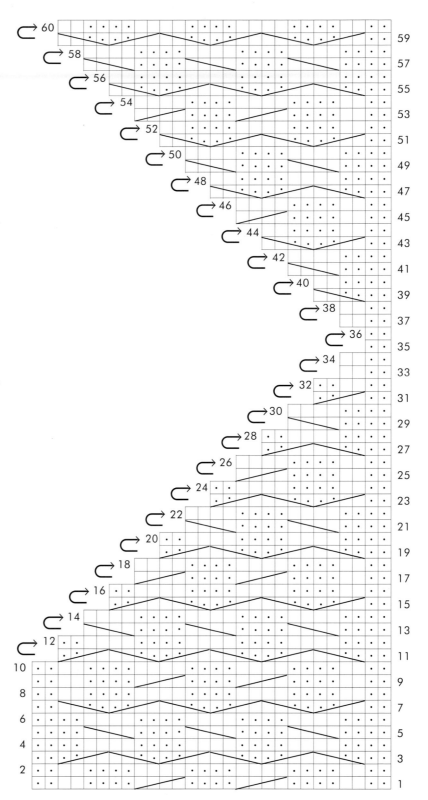

Reading the Charts

I have expressed the patterns in this book as charts, because, once you get used to the symbols, the chart becomes a graphic representation of the knitting with the general shape of the pattern clearly visible. It's easy to keep track of where you are in the pattern as you knit, and to see exactly what to do next, as the squares placed above one another on the chart correspond exactly to the sts above one another in the knitting.

Every square in the charts corresponds to a stitch and a row in the knitting. The numbers along the side of the chart show the number of the row. Read each row from the side the number is on. On the front of the work, read the chart from right to left, and on the wrong side of work, read from left to right.

In most of the patterns in this book, the sts on the wrong side of the work are knitted as they appear on your needles — knit into knit sts, purl into purl, except for the row with the final decreases and the first row after the ribbing.

The chart shows how the pattern looks from the front, the outside, which stitches should appear knit or purl, which are laid in front of others as cables or traveling sts. This is accomplished with the help of symbols in the squares. Please be aware then, that the same symbol is knitted differently on a knit (right side) or a purl (wrong side) row of the work. There is a key to the symbols on the last page.

Please also note that most of the charts have a number of black squares. These are included because of increases and decreases in the pattern, which means that the number of stitches in the chart actually changes. For the appearance of the chart to match the knitting, black squares were drawn on the rows

with fewer sts so that all the stitches have the same vertical position relative tine on both sides and the number of sts in the repeat are given underneath. When there are two numbers, the lower number gives the number of stitches without the increases in the pattern and the higher number tells the number of stitches *including* the increases for the pattern.

The portion of the pattern which should *not* be repeated is found outside the heavy lines.

Vertically, each chart has a number of rows to be repeated, also called a "repeat." Most often, all the rows are to be repeated. Rows numbered "0" are to be knitted only once or the number of times indicated in the text. Panels of pattern can be varied by lengthening the "straightaway", most often Rows 1-2 or Row 1-4, between motifs.

There are also some patterns which are knitted with short rows

(See p. 120). In that case, the chart shows only the stitches which will actually be knitted, and arrows show where to turn within the work.

Allover patterns are repeated both vertically and horizontally. Panels are repeated either vertically or horizontally, and solitary motifs are placed following the directions and are not repeated.

When you cast on sts, count only the knit and purl sts in the chart, and ignore increase signs and black squares.

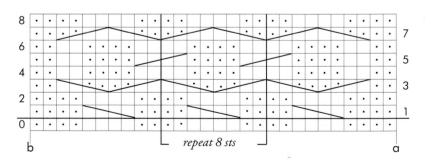

repeat 8 sts

Traveling Stitches and Cable Crosses

In order to knit any of the patterns in this book you must know how to knit cables. Only six different cable crosses are used, and all are presented in this section. Because no more than four stitches are involved in any of the cable crossings in this book, once you have the basics, all the patterns will be fairly easy to knit.

All the patterns are based on cable-style crossing of stitches, where two knit stitches cross over one or two other stitches, which can be either knit or purl.

The simplest is the classic cable cross involving four stitches, two crossing over two, either to the right or the left. The others are in principle done the same way.

Crossing 4 knit stitches to the right

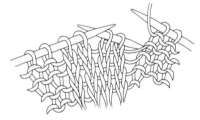

Set 2 stitches on a short needle (or "cable needle") and pull them behind the work, knit the next 2 stitches,

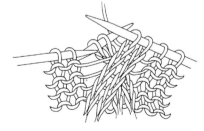

then knit the two stitches from the cable needle.

Crossing 4 knit stitches to the left

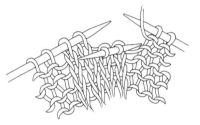

Put two k stitches on a short knitting needle (or "cable needle") and bring them to front of work,

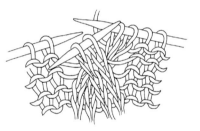

knit the next two stitches, then knit the two stitches on the short needle.

Cross two knit stitches over two purl stitches, to right, by following the directions for crossing two knit stitches to the right, but purl the two stitches on the short needle: Put two stitches on a short needle and bring behind the work, knit the next two stitches, purl the two stitches on the short needle.

Cross two knits over two purls to the left by following directions for crossing four knit stitches, but purl the first two stitches before knitting the stitches from the short needle.

Put two stitches on a short needle and bring to front of work, purl the next two stitches, then knit the stitches on the short needle.

Cross two knits over one purl, to right

Put one stitch on a short needle, behind the work, knit the next two stitches, then purl the stitch from the short needle.

Cross two knits over one purl, to left

Put two stitches on a short needle and bring to front of work, purl the next st, then knit the short needle's two stitches.

For an experienced knitter who doesn't knit tightly, it's entirely possible to make these crosses without using a cable needle.

The New Technique: How to Do It

Besides their connection to the Viking period and its ornamentation, the patterns between these covers have one thing in common: It has never been possible to knit them before.

They are all based on a technical innovation, an old technique used in an entirely new way. Here it is unveiled—with careful directions to show you how actually to do it.

We're not really talking about a knit-technical *invention*. The technique itself isn't new. At least, the way to lean an increase or a decrease to the right or left has been known for a long time. The news is in how to use these increases and decreases in textured knitting.

Cables consist of crossed stitches. These crossings pull the work up, so that the number of stitches per inch in an all-over cable pattern is greater than the number of stitches in ordinary stockinette—and reverse stockinette is most often used as a background for cables. To start a cable in the middle of a project, one has to increase within the cable pattern to compensate, or there will be bulges in the reverse stockinette background.

For a single cable or a horizontal band of vertical cables, one can increase at the cable or spread increases evenly across the work to to compensate. But the complicated pattern panels and allover patterns shown here, with frequent starts and stops within the motifs themselves, call for a handier and more localized method of increasing and decreasing.

What *is* new is actually two things: the mirrored, directional increases, which make it possible to increase in placement of the increases and corresponding decreases, which make possible to close off a cable attractively.

This chapter reviews the increases and decreases systematically, and the order to knit them in, because, even if the technique itself is known, its application isn't general knowledge.

Increases

Increases are always made in pairs and to the right in the next stitch, to the left in the stitch just knitted. The stitch increased *in* is called the "base stitch." All increases are on the front of the work.

1 Increasing to the left on reverse stockinette

Purl up to the increase symbol on the chart. You have already purled the base stitch. Carry your yarn to the back, and with the left needle lift the purl loop from two rows *under* the base stitch. (It appears directly beneath the yarn from your last stitch.) Knit the purl loop.

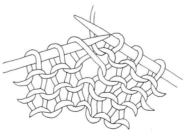

The increase is completed. On the

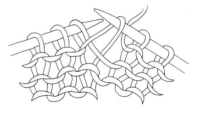

next row, working on the back side, purl the increase st so it will show up as a knit stitch on the front.

2 Right increase on reverse stockinette

Purl up to the increase sign on the chart. Bring working yarn to back of work. With the right needle lift the purl loop from under the next stich (from the previous row). (The purl loop is on the right side of work.)

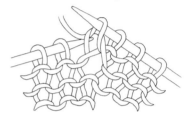

Knit the loop.

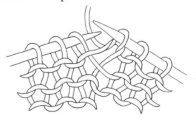

The increase is completed. Now purl the base stitch (the stitch you have just pulled the purl loop from under). On the next row, on the back of work, purl the increased stitch.

3 Left increase on stockinette (knit stitches)

Knit up to the increase sign. The base stitch has already been knitted. With the left needle, lift the purl loop (behind the work) from two rows under the base stitch just knitted. It will be the first loop *under* your working yarn on back of work.

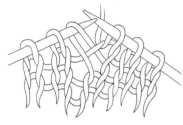

Knit the loop.

The increase is now completed. On the next row, from the back side of work, purl the increased stitch (and all the others).

4 Right increase on stockinette (knit stitches)

Knit up to the increase sign on the chart. With the right needle, lift the purl loop from the previous row, from under and behind the next stitch.

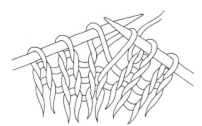

Knit the loop.

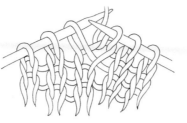

The increase is complete. Now knit the base stitch (the next stitch). In the next row, working on the back side, purl the increased stitch (and all the others as well).

The Lillbjärs panel is an exception, in that the increase must come a row later. This is done on the back side, in purl stitches, but is essentially the same procedure: Increase by lifting the purl loop from under the next stitch, but the increase must be purled to show up as a knit on the right side of work. These increases, like the others, are made every second row.

Placement of increases

A paired increase consists of a left increase placed right next to a right increase. In braided and knotted patterns, paired increases require two steps.

Both increases are made on reverse stockinette on right side of the work. The first increase is done made on reverse stockinette (the background) and the next is in the next right side row, between the first two increase stitches, thus, between two knit stitches.

Decreases

In these sweaters I used only two different decreases. They are mirror image and are used in pairs in the patterning.

The first is simply to knit two stitches together, which produces a decrease that leans to the right on the right side of the work. The other is the "pass the slipped stitch over" decrease, (PSSO) which leans to the left.

On the back of the work, the decreases are made in the same way. Knit a knit and a purl stitch together, and the last two stitches of a cable will disappear. The decreased stitches appear as purl stitches on the right side of the work.

Of course, one could simply use one kind of decrease, knit two together, on the back of the work, but using mirrored decreases make the back of the work look neater.

Passing the slipped stitch over (PSSO), front of work

Slip the first stitch knitwise onto right needle. In the drawing this has already happened.

Knit the next stitch and lift the slipped stitch over it.

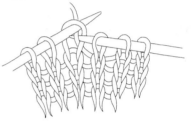

On the right side, two knit stitches will be decreased this way. On the wrong side, it would be a knit and a purl.

(Translator's note: **Slip, Slip, Knit (SSK)** I have widely substituted the Slip, Slip, Knit (SSK) decrease for PSSO, partly because it is familiar to American knitters and slants in the same direction as PSSO decreases, and partly because the Swedish abbreviation for PSSO decreases includes stitches that must be expressed in English—i.e., slip 1, k 1, PSSO = Swedish *öhpt*,—making the pattern text bulkier and more confusing. SSK means: slip one stitch knitwise, slip next stitch knitwise, replace left needle in both stitches from back and knit together (developed by Elizabeth Zimmermann).)

Knit two stitches together, knit side of work (Knit 2 together)

On the front of the work, there are two knit sts to be knitted together. On the back of the work, there is a knit and a purl stitch.

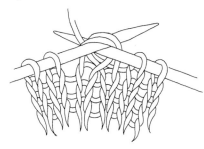

Purl two stitches together (purl 2 together)

Purl two purl stitches together by inserting right needle through first st purlwise, then second stitch purlwise. Purl.

Twist two purl stitches together (Twist 2 purl stitches together)

Go behind the next two stitches, insert right needle into both stitches from the back side, and purl.

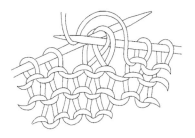

These increases and decreases are fine to use in shaping garments as well and are especially useful when the shaping has to happen in a single row, as they provide left and right facing options that look alike from the front of the garment.

Placement of decreases

In knotted and closed cable patterns, decreases are made in two steps. The first decrease is made on the front of the work. The first two knit stitches are decreased PSSO (or SSK), the second two are knitted together.

The other decrease is on the back of the work: slip the last st of the background (which will be a knit stitch on the back of the work) knitwise, k the first st of the cable strand and pass the slipped st over it. Knit the next two stitches (a purl and a knit) together. These two stitches will show as purl stitches on the right side and will become part of the purled background.

On the Lillbjärs panel, the decreases come one row earlier. The first decrease is made on the back side of the work: Purl two purl stitches together, then twist two purl stitches together. The second decrease is on the right side of work. Use the same purled decrease as the first.

This paired decrease makes a less pointed close on loops in the pattern and the shape better matches that of the increases below. The wrong side decrease is much harder to knit than the one on the right side, and you can decide yourself whether it's worth the effort. In the Lillbjärs panel, however, it was necessary in order to keep the increases and decreases from running together.

Tricks (and Tips) of the Trade

This chapter is about getting good results with my patterns. I pass on my experiences with methods and techniques that make knitting easier and will help you to be successful and happy with what you knit. I go through the most important elements of the patterns and clarify a few details that may not be self explanatory.

I've tried to make my directions clear and easily understandable, but they assume that you have certain basic skills, and much is unstated in the directions.

A set of knitting directions has three parts. The first, the factual part, tells everything you need to begin to knit, and the conditions you need to get good results. The second part is a set of step-by-step directions, which tell you how to knit the article. The third has directions for assembling and finishing the garment.

Always read through the entire set of directions before you start to knit.

Part 1: The facts

Size, measurements, and yarn

The first information given is size and the measurements of the garment. Don't lock yourself into a size before you consider which size has measurements that match your figure and taste. You might also measure a favorite sweater as a basis for your choice. The sizes are given from smallest to largest and every second number is set in parentheses to make them easy to read. Where there is only one number, it applies to all the sizes.

It's a good idea to circle or highlight the numbers in the directions that apply to your size before you start to knit. Then it's easier to find the right ones.

Here is also found the kind of yarn used and how much you will need.

Tension and needle size

Tension—How many stitches you knit per 4 inches/10 cm—is the most important element in the directions. Pay attention to your tension! If your knitting tension doesn't match the directions, the measurements won't match either.

So, the first commandment of knitting is *knit a tension swatch!*

Using the yarn you plan to use on the garment and the needles recommended, knit your tension swatch. It should measure about 4 inches/10 x 10 cm plus selvage stitches. On it, you then measure how many stitches you have knitted in 4 inches/10 cm in width (stitch tension) and how many rows you have knitted in 4 inches/10 cm of height (row tension). Usually, there are more rows per measure than stitches per measure (in plain stockinette, about 3 rows for every 2 stitches).

The needle size given is only a recommendation and is based on an average knitter, but getting the correct stitch tension is much more important than using the same needle size. If you knit more loosely (too few stitches per 4 inches/10 cm), change to a thinner (lower number) knitting needle. If you knit more tightly (too many stitches per 4 inches/10 cm), move to a thicker (higher number) needle size. Then knit another tension swatch until the number of stitches per measure matches the tension in the directions. In my directions, I always give the tension in stockinette first. My experience is that if the tension matches in stockinette, it will also match in pattern knitting. However, as this is not infallible, I also often give a tension for the pattern panel, which gives the knitter a little extra check on how things are going.

Selvage stitches

The outside stitch on both sides is always knitted—on both right and wrong sides—and is the selvage stitch.

It makes an even finish on sides and collars and functions also as a seam allowance.

The boundary between the pattern and the selvage stitch is clearly marked and permits exact seams, especially where there are increases and decreases just inside the selvage stitch.

Ribbing is knitted without selvage stitches, so that the seam will lie flatter. The selvage stitch is always counted into the number of cast-on stitches. When it's not indicated in the chart, knit the outermost square of the chart as a selvage stitch, and—except on ribbing—the selvage stitch is a knit stitch on both sides, no matter what the chart shows.

Part 2: Knitting directions

Normally, the back is presented first, probably because it takes a while for the pattern to "take hold" in your hands and possible problem spots are less noticeable in back. However, if the front has a different pattern panel that may affect the length, the front is given first.

All instructions are carried out on the front of the work or beginning on the front, if not indicated otherwise.

All length measurements are taken with the knitting hanging down. This is how the length will be when you wear the garment, and with some yarns it makes a difference.

Cast-ons and other edgings

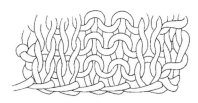

Cast on with two needles held together to get an even and stretchable edge. All the patterns are cast on with the most ordinary long tail cast on. (In Swedish, it's even called "school cast-on.") It's flexible and gives a nice edge

with a twined look on one side. Because this smooth, twined edge should always be on the outside, the second row is always on the inside, or wrong side, of the work.

Ribbed and garter stitch edgings and hems are ordinarily knitted with finer needles than the rest of the garment.

When the pattern begins directly following the cast-on, the first row (wrong side) is knitted as a setting-up row following Row 0 or the *last* row of the chart, after which you knit Row 1 on the chart as the first row of the right side.

Ribbing

When the first row is knit one, purl one ribbing, and it's on the wrong side of the work, the row begins "knit 1, purl 1" on an odd number of stitches. That way, there is automatically always a knit stitch on both ends just inside the outermost stitch *on the right side of the work* and the seam is easier to sew up neatly.

With knit 2, purl 2 ribbing, the first row begins with "purl 2" on the wrong side, and a multiple of 4 + 2 stitches, which makes the row also end with purl 2. The first and last stitches are considered selvage stitches but, in this case, the seam will be flatter if they're knitted in stockinette. The seam lies one stitch in from the edge, hiding the selvage stitch and creating 2 knit stitches side by side at the seam, on the right side.

Decreasing

Decrease at the armhole and neck edges and for the sleeve cap every other row if not indicated otherwise. Decrease within the selvage stitches at the beginning of the row by knitting 2 together in stockinette or 2 twisted together in reverse stockinette. Decrease inside the selvage stitch at the end of the row by PSSO or SSK in stockinette and by purling 2 together in reverse stockinette. (See pp. 113-

114 for details.)

These decrease techniques can also be used for reducing 3 stitches to one.

Increasing

Increases are also made inside the selvage stitches and are most often on the right side of the work. It's a good idea to use directional increases and to increase to the right at the beginning of the row and to the left at the end of the row (See pages 112-113 for details.). Never increase in the selvage stitches!

On the sleeves, you are often asked to increase alternately on the fourth and sixth rows. You could certainly increase every fifth row, but then every second increase would be on a purl row. If, for whatever reason—looser rows or shorter arms—you haven't room for all the increases for the sleeves, you can group them more closely at the top, say every second row, in order to get them all in.

In designs with set in sleeves, be sure to knit all increases called for, or you risk having a sleeve cap too small for the arm hole. In a dropped shoulder design with no sleeve cap, it's okay to leave out a few increases if you're sure the sleeve is wide enough at the top.

"Place marker"

I use a length of contrasting yarn as a marker.

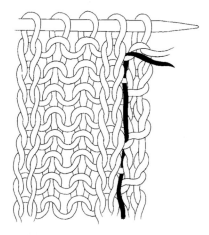

I use different colors to mark different events. For example, I use red to mark increases and decreases on the sides, and I use blue to mark off repeats of the pattern. I do the actual marking by laying the contrast yarn between two stitches from front to back and later back again.

The marker then runs like a basting stitch up through the project. Every time it switches sides in the work, something has occurred, and I can immediately see when I increased last and how many increases I have made. If I'm not sure where to start knitting after taking a break, I only need to count the number of rows since the beginning of the last repeat. Keeping count like this makes the knitting seem to go faster and makes it easier to get various pieces the same length.

"Put stitches on holder"— a contrasting yarn

At the neckline you're told to put the center stitches on a holder and knit the sides separately. By putting them on a holder instead of binding them off, you make the transition between the body and the neckline smoother and the neck itself more elastic. I myself usually bind off, but in a piece of scrap yarn in a contrasting color. It's then easy to block the pieces before assembling them without worrying about a holder, as well as being a snap to pick up the stitches while ripping out the bind-off. In this case, ripping will be easier if you decreased: k 2 together, *slip st from right needle knitwise onto left needle, k 2 together,* repeating this across the row.

Binding off

Bind off for these patterns by "knit 2 together," pass the first stitch over the second, knit another stitch, pass the remaing stitch over it, etc. When you bind off edges that will be visible, it's important to bind off in pattern, that is, knit stitches should be knitted and purl stitches should be purled, even on the bind off row.

When you bind off circularly, for example on a neckband, and want as smooth a line as possible, you can avoid "stair steps" by slipping the first stitch without knitting it, then binding off as usual. Binding off should be done consistently, neither too tightly nor too loosely.

Part 3: Assembly

Assembly is an all-important element of knitting a garment. A sloppy job of assembling can ruin even the best knitting job, and a great assembly can rescue uneven knitting.

So, take your time and do the assembly carefully, even if it seems tedious and is not knitting. In each pattern, only that which is unique to that particular pattern is presented with the overall directions. There's more.

Work in tails

It goes without saying that all loose ends—tails—should be fastened down, and invisibly. Usually I leave long tails when casting on and at the shoulders to use in sewing up the garment.

Join new strands of yarn at edges to be sewn. Later, get rid of the tail by running it in and out of the selvage stitches.

"Block all pieces to measure"

This means to spread out each piece of the garment in its correct shape. Then pin, very closely, around all the edges. Check that the measurements match those in the directions and that the knitting is laid out straight. Lay a damp towel over them, or spray lightly with water in a plant spray bottle.

A good way to block is to lay the two sleeves on top of each other and the front(s) on top of the back, but pin them individually, and spray between the layers. In this way, everything that should be the same shape, will be.

Let the whole sandwich lie until bone dry. Blocking reduces the width-wise curl in the knitting and makes sewing up easier. Blocking also evens out lumpiness in the knit.

A good base for blocking is a 31½ x 47½ in (80 x 120 cm) fiberboard covered with a light cotton fabric, easily stored behind a door. Checked fabric, mounted square, helps in measuring and shaping. A folded blanket covered with a towel also makes a good blocking base.

"Sew shoulder seams"

The shoulder seams come out flatter and more flexible if you knit, rather than sew, them together, and the pattern will automatically match perfectly.

Pick up the shoulder stitches on two needles so that the points face in the same direction when the pieces are laid right sides facing. Knit two stitches, one from each needle, together. Knit another two stitches together and pass the first stitch over the second—that is, bind off the stitches as they come onto the right needle.

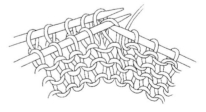

The tops of hoods are also knitted together. Shoulder seams finished this way sometimes stretch. To avoid this, either run a strong thread through the shoulder seam to keep it in shape, or bind off each piece separately and graft the seam using Kitchener stitch (below).

"Pick up stitches"

Always pick up stitches from the right side of the work if not instructed otherwise.

I prefer to knit neckbands on circular needles and the number of stitches given is calculated for that. If you are knitting flat, place the seam at the left shoulder and add selvage stitches (depending on the pattern) so that your seam will be invisible.

Sewing up the right shoulder seam first is an old tailoring rule, which probably has to do with most of us being right handed and that the right half of the body is usually more visible.

When picking up front edge stitches for ribbing, pick up into the stitches *inside* the selvage stitch. A good rule of thumb is to pick up a stitch each from 2 rows and skip the third row. Or, pick up stitches in 3 rows and skip the fourth. By purling the first row (on the wrong side) and then beginning the ribbing, you can avoid the tendency of the front to roll toward the purl side. Bind off the edge in pattern, that is, knit into knit stitches, purl into purl, on the bind-off row.

Seams

Side and underarm seams can be sewn either with vertical grafting from the right side (see right), or with a back stitch on the wrong side. Sew ribbing together with vertical grafting. Ribbing in these designs is calculated so that two knit stitches meet on the sides.

On reverse stockinette, vertical grafting is less noticeable than any other seam, although not strictly invisible.

If you choose to sew the shoulder seams together, use Kitchener stitch (shown lower right), also called "grafting."

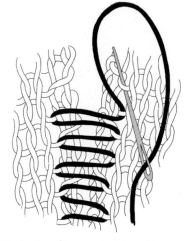

Vertical grafting on (knit) stockinette

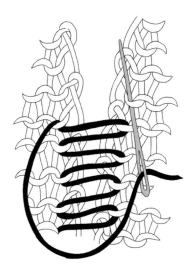

Vertical grafting on reverse stockinette

Front edges and collars are best sewn on with grafting, so you can see what you're doing. Straight sleeves on dropped shoulders can be sewn with vertical grafting. Here you will find that the number of stitches doesn't quite work with the number of rows without first pinning (or basting) carefully first and then sewing one stitch to alternately one and two rows. Use grafting also for seams where it's important that the patterns match.

Inset sleeves with caps are always sewn in with backstitch so that they have the right shape.

Buttonholes

The simplest way to knit buttonholes is to—at the desired position—bind off 2-4 stitches and on the following row to cast on the same number over the hole. I prefer one-row buttonholes. I describe here a buttonhole 2 stitches wide, but the same method can be used no matter how many stitches you need in your buttonhole.

Knit up to the 2 stitches that will form the buttonhole. Slip the first stitch onto the right needle, pass the second stitch on the left needle over the

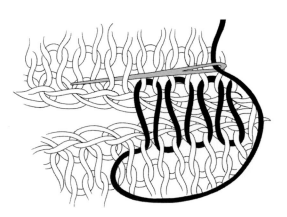

Horizontal grafting, also called Kitchener Stitch.

first. Place the slipped stitch back on the left needle and pass the stitch which is now the second stitch over the first. Knit the stitch which is now the first on the left needle.

Cast on two more stitches. The drawing shows simple thumb cast-ons, or half-hitches. The buttonhole is finished.

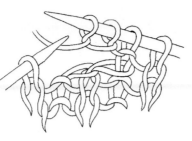

Joining a new strand of yarn

There are a number of different ways to join a new strand of yarn. A simple way is to join the new yarn at the end of a row. Knot the two ends there, and later, when you have sewn the seam, thread the tails into the seam allowance. *Never* join a new yarn at the front edge, only at edges that are to be sewn together. If the yarn is two- or four-ply, you can split the plies apart, break one side of each shorter, reassemble the yarn with one half from each end, and knit three to five stitches with the combination.

Lining

If you wish to line a garment, you can use the parts you have knitted as a pattern. Leave generous seam allowances and ideally, make a pleat in the back, as cloth is less flexible than knitting. The lining should stop and be tacked down at the top of the ribbing.

ABBREVIATIONS
k = knit
p = purl
inc, incs = increase, increases
dec, decs = decrease, decreases
st, sts = stitch, stitches
rnd = round, the equivalent of "row" when knitting circularly

Short Rows

Short rows, or partial rows, are a technique to shape knitted fabric by knitting some rows only partially, then turning and knitting back within the same space. These rows are therefore shorter than the others, and bulge outward in one direction or another—useful for socks, yokes, turning corners, and other applications.

For example, I slope shoulders with short rows and in that way get smoother shoulder line and a flatter shoulder seam. Short rows can also be used to knit darts for the bust, to raise the back of a pair of pants, and to give better shape to a sweater with a circularly knit yoke.

If you turn around in the middle of a row, a little hole will show where you turned: the point where you turned is two rows higher than the other side of that point. This can be used to decorative effect, but sometimes that doesn't fit into your plans. The little hole can be taken care of in two ways. Both are good but only in different circumstances.

The easiest way, wrapping, is also the most useful and can be done on either the knit or the purl side and regardless of what pattern you're knitting. It results in a little horizontal line in the knit, which is, however, hardly noticeable on reverse stockinette or on small texture patterns like moss stitch.

Knit right up to the point where you will turn, bring the working yarn behind the work and slip the next st. Bring the working yarn behind the slipped stitch and forward to the front of the work, and slip the stitch, choked by its neck, back onto the left needle. Turn and knit back. The "little horizontal line" can be avoided by, in the next row, knitting *under* the wrapping loop and knitting it together

with the stitch above it. This is the method used to fill out the shoulders in *Fjalar.*

The other way is especially suited for ribbing, and I used it to get a good shaping of the collar on *Rafn.* Knit up to the turning point. Turn, yarn over, and knit back.

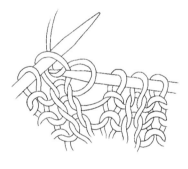

In the next row, knit the yarn over and the following stitch together.

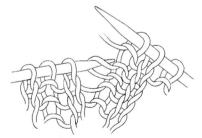

Yarn-over and the stitch it will be knitted together with.

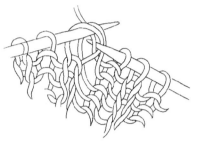

Knitting together the yarn over and the next stitch.

In this way, the yarn-over will be hidden behind the knit stitch. The turn must always lie between a purl and a knit stitch, with the last stitch before turning, a purl stitch and therefore the first stitch after the turn, a knit stitch. Otherwise, the knitting together of the yarn-over and the next stitch, which you will do the next time you encounter them, will not be invisible.

When you knit two mirror-image pieces, like two halves of a collar, the turn will lie at different points on the two halves, depending on whether you knit the yarnover and its following stitch together on the right or the wrong side of the work.

In the designs using short rows in this book, I've made the short rows successively shorter so that you can knit all the yarnovers and their following stitches together in one row.

Sizes and Fit

When designing a garment, I try to attain a harmony between the shape of the garment, the pattern, and the color and character of the yarn. Because of this, some of the garments are given in only one size. Those who need a larger or smaller size, or want to alter the shape somehow, should read the following tips.

In many of these designs, the knots and plaiting patterns have controlled the size. I would much rather preserve the pattern whole than break a panel, for example, to have the correct shoulder width. Instead, I've found other solutions, as in *Harald*, where I placed an extra rib in the side of the yoke to get enough width under the armhole in some sizes.

In other sweaters, such solutions didn't work, and the sweater is then given in only one size. The measurements can still be altered another way, by changing your knitting tension—knitting looser or tighter. The assumptions are that the yarn can stand being knitted more loosely—that is, there is no risk of the garment losing its shape—and that the sweater itself is not too closely fitted.

By knitting more tightly or loosely, you not only change your stitch tension, and thereby, the width of the garment, you also change the row tension, and with it, the length of the garment. The result in such a case can be a complete rewrite of the directions. Straight garments, on the other hand, don't have problems like this and can be freely altered.

Ragna can be made smaller if you knit with needles a half (metric) size smaller and a tension of 17 sts = 4 inches or 10 cm. The bust measurement will then be about 44¾ in/114 cm. If you want to make it larger, use needles a half (metric) size larger and a stitch tension of 15 sts = 4 inches/10 cm, which will give a bust measurement of 49½ in/126 cm.

Hermod's size can be adjusted in the same way. At a tension of 17 sts = 4 inches or 10 cm, the chest measurement becomes 44 in/112 cm. At 15 sts = 4 inches or 10 cm becomes 50¼ in/128 cm.

The chest measurement of *Fjörgyn* can be reduced by knitting at a tension of 13 sts = 4 inches or 10 cm, bringing chest measurement to 47¼ in/120 cm.

On all these designs, the depth of the armhole is affected by several centimeters. The sweater length is also affected if you want the same arrangement of the pattern panels as I have, but this can be adjusted as you wish.

In designs like those above and *Vigdis* and *Harald*, shaping is irrelevant, and changing the chest measurement is adequate.

You can knit the sleeves as long as you wish. Most sleeves can be lengthened quite simply by continuing to knit even at the top until they are long enough. If you shorten a sleeve, however, you can find yourself at the top of the sleeve before you've made all the increases called for. It's all right to pack the remaining increases together in the last few rows before the top.

If you want to lengthen *Frode*, the best way is to add extra rows before, after, and between the happiness signs,

while *Hervor* should be lengthened by adding rows immediately after the ribbing.

To lengthen or shorten *Rafn*, knit, or eliminate, a half motif at the top, so that two half motifs meet at the shoulder. The jacket will then be 2-2½ inches (5-6 cm) shorter or longer. If you'd rather not have a shawl collar, you can knit a V-neck instead: Continue knitting the selvage stitches and decrease for the neck as indicated in the directions. In that case, ignore the increases for the collar and its shaping.

The two closely fitted designs, *Freja* and *Vebjörg*, can be neither lengthened nor shortened without dire consequences to the pattern panels. On the other hand, it works fine to eliminate the shaping on the sides and knit these two sweaters straight up.

Adjusting tension and lengths can affect the amount of yarn you will need, so be sure you buy enough yarn of the same dye lot before you start.

Yarn

I have used mostly natural fibers for the garments in this book. Natural fibers are beautiful, they retain their beauty even through many washings, and they age with grace.

The yarns were carefully chosen, both to complement the pattern and the character of the garment. This section is to warn you against changing yarns—and to give you some tips should you choose to ignore my warnings!

Wool yarn is best for knitting plaited patterns. Wool has a good elasticity that makes knitting easy, and it "fills" well, creating an even background and making the braiding stand out boldly.

The heavier yarns are untreated, which gives them a coarseness and a rustic character, both of which I treasure.

The lighter sweaters are knitted in a wool yarn which has been super-wash treated, and thus are machine washable. The treatment also reduces the risk of scratchiness—of interest if you're planning to wear the sweater without undergarments.

Rafn is knitted in alpaca yarn, which has more luster than wool, drapes more heavily, and is warmer.

Some sweaters are knitted in a silk/wool blend. Silk has no elasticity in itself, but blended with wool it becomes easier to knit and the yarn acquires some of the softness and luster of the silk.

Silk is an environmentally friendly fiber, partly because the silkworms are sensitive to any kind of pollution. Silk is therefore seldom treated at any stage with chemicals.

Hermod is knitted of a recycled yarn, that is ravelled-up second-hand fiber which is then spun into yarn with a small percentage of new wool fibers. This yarn contains some cotton. It is therefore less elastic and less lustrous than yarn made of new fibers.

You can of course knit any of these garments in other yarns than the ones suggested. In the yarn suppliers list both the fiber blend and the yardage per weight is given, which should be helpful when switching yarns.

However, be aware that these are only two of the factors involved. The breed of sheep, which part of the sheep the wool comes from, even the climate the sheep lived in, can affect the quality of wool yarn. Silk fiber taken from the outside of the cocoon is different from silk taken from the inside of the cocoon. The length and thickness of each fiber, the ply, whether the yarn is hard or loose spun, and post-spinning treatments are all factors that give specific yarns their own qualities.

For these reasons there's no guarantee that two yarns will behave in the same way even though they have the same yardage/lb and the same stated fiber content. If you change to a completely different fiber—say, from wool to cotton—a lot can happen. In this case, the ribbing would lose all elasticity.

A bit of advice if you want to use a different yarn: knit a substantial sample swatch in the desired pattern, then see and feel if you're happy with the result.

Care of Knitted Garments

A fine, hand-knitted garment is worth caring for. Properly handled, it can become part of the inheritance you pass on to coming generations. When one speaks, as I do here, of garments in a tradition more than a thousand years old, it's reasonable to include some suggestions for maintaining and preserving the different fibers they're made of.

Wool tends to shed dirt, so you needn't wash wool garments often. If the garment doesn't get extremely dirty, one wash per season is probably adequate. Instead, if it needs refreshing, dampen it lightly. This particularly applies to heavier sweaters not worn directly against the skin. Both detergent/soap and mechanical washing of any kind wears on the fiber. Even from an environmental standpoint, it's important to wash a garment no more than necessary.

Wash the garment with the wrong side out. This reduces the wear on the outside as well as pilling and felting.

Handwash in lukewarm water. Be careful that the rinse water and the wash water are the same temperature. Wool can tolerate fairly warm temperatures, if it's warmed up slowly, but not sudden temperature changes. After the final hand rinse, spin in the washing machine for about 30 seconds, or squeeze out the water by hand.

Do not wring and do not scrub. If you work wool too vigorously, it will shrink and felt, especially if you are using a strong, basic soap or detergent. Use neutral ph value detergents or soaps intended for silk or wool, dish detergent, or shampoo. Adding a spoonful of vinegar to the last rinse helps the fibers retain their luster and strength. Mild acid strengthens wool fibers.

Wash silk the same way as wool.

Superwash wool can be machine washed on the wool program. Even so, use a mild detergent.

Spread the clean garment on a towel, ease it into its correct shape, and let it dry flat.

Always follow washing directions on the yarn wrapper.

Always wash knitted garments with the wrong side out.

Dry and store knitted garments flat (never on a hanger).

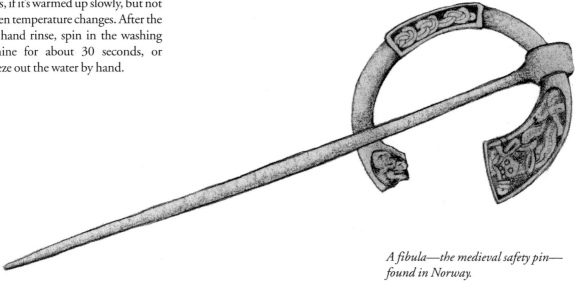

A fibula—the medieval safety pin—found in Norway.

Photos

Antikvarisk-Topografiska Arkivet (ATA)
Horse figure from Birka, Uppland (Sweden), p. 58
Sword hilt from Ultuna, Uppland (Sweden), p. 68
Calendar staff from Nyköping, Södermanland (Sweden), p. 101

ATA/H. Faith-Ell
Picture stone from Lillbjärs, Gotland (Sweden), pp. 32, 88

Luzzi Herzog
Runestones, rune slabs, pp. 92, 102, 103

Nationalmuseet, Copenhagen/Kit Weiss
Gold buckle, Hornelund, Denmark, p. 33

Oslo Universitets Oldsakssamling/E.I. Johnson
Chair from Tylldal Kirke, Tynset, Hedmark, Norway, p. 44

Anders Rydell
Stone cross from Brompton, Yorkshire, England, p. 11
Picture stone from York, England, p. 12
Also, black and white pattern swatches

York Archeological Trust/Simon I. Hill
Helmet from Coppergate, York, England, p. 90

Finlands Nationalmuseum/Timo Syrjänen
Sword from Pappilanmäki, Finland, p. 73

Artifacts

Sweden: 43 objects:
Uppland: pp. 13, 14, 15, 19, 27 (detail), 35 (2pcs.), 58 (2 pcs.), 59, 63, 63 (detail), 68, 71 (detail), 87, 89, 92, 99, 102, 103.
Gotland: pp. 9, 13, 23 (detail), 27, 32 (detail), 36, 40, 42, 54, 68, 72, 88, 91, 102.
Skåne: pp. 34, 50, 93.
Småland: pp.10, 34.
Södermanland: pp. 69, 101.
Östergötland: pp. 2, 48.
Norrbotten: p. 30.
Närke: p. 31.

Norway: 12 objects: pp. 13, 22, 27, 44, 45, 72, 96, 100, 102, 103, 107 (2 pcs.).

England: 8 objects: pp. 11, 12, 22, 41 (2 pcs.), 44, 90, 95.

Denmark: 5 objects: pp. 32, 33, 41, 58, 103.

Finland: 1 object, p. 73.

Ireland: 1 object, p. 42.

Iceland: 1 object, p. 102.

Yarn Information & Suppliers

from Charisma: ***Evergreen Collection Cotton Lambswool***, 45 % cotton, 45 % lambswool, 10 % other fibers of which 80 % are recycled fiber, 20 % virgin wool. 50 g = 69 m.
Evergreen Collection Cotton Lambswool is available in Sweden from the manufacturer.

from Garnstudio: ***Silketweed***, 50 % silk, 50 % wool. 50 g = 200 m.
Silketweed is available in the United States from Aurora Yarns and the Yarn Barn and in Sweden from the manufacturer.

from Gepard: ***Lord of Aran***, 100 % wool. 100 g = 150 m.
Soft Woolsilk, 70 % wool, 30 % silk. 50 g = 175 m.
Gepard yarns are available in Sweden from Ingen Konst.

from Istex: ***Lopi***, 100 % wool. 100 g = 100 m.
Lopi is available in the United States from Halcyon Yarn, JCA Inc., Patternworks, Schoolhouse Press, The Wool Room, and Yarn Barn and in Sweden from Järbo Garn.

from Klippans Yllefabrik: ***Fjord***, 100 % wool, superwash. 50 g = 125 m.
Fjord is available in Sweden from the manufacturer.

from Naturgarn: ***Alpacka Sport***, 100% alpaca. 100 g = 150 m.
U84, 100 % wool. 100 g = 200 m.
Alpaca Sport is available in the United States from Patternworks. *Alpacka Sport* and *U84* are available in Sweden from the manufacturer.

from Rowan: ***Magpie Tweed***, 100 % wool. 100 g = 150 m.
Chunky Tweed, 100 % wool. 100 g = 100 m.
DK Tweed, 100 % wool. 50 g = 135 m.
Rowan yarns are available in the United States from Westmisnter Fibers and the Yarn Barn and in Sweden from Wincent.

from Uldvarefabrik: ***Smart***, 100 % wool, superwash. 50 g = 100 m.
Smart is available in the United States from the Fabric Place and from Patternworks by special order. *Smart* is available in Sweden from Almedahls.

from Yllet: ***Yllets Ullgarn 3***, 100 % wool. 100 g = 200 m.
Yllets Ullgarn 3 is available in Sweden from the manufacturer.

American Suppliers

Aurora Yarns
P.O. Box 3068
Moss Beach, CA 94038
650-728-2730

Bea Ellis Knitwear
P.O. Box 1188
Marshfield, MA 02050
781-837-1750

Fabric Place
Woburn Mall
300 Mishawum Rd.
Woburn, MA 01801
781-938-8787

Halcyon Yarn
3 School Street
Bath, ME 04530
207-442-7909

JCA, Inc.
35 Scales Lane
Townsend, MA 01469
978-597-8794

Nordic Fiber Arts
4 Cutts Road
Durham, NH 03824
603-868-1196

Patternworks
36 S. Gate Drive #A
Poughkeepsie, NY 12601
914-462-8000

Schoolhouse Press
6899 Carybluff
Pittsville, WI 54466
715-884-2799

Westminster Fibers
5 Northern Boulevard
Amherst, NH 03031
603-886-5041

The Wool Room
218 Pleasant Street
Antrim, NH 03440
603-588-6637

Yarn Barn
930 Massachusetts Street
Lawrence, KS 66044
800-468-0035

Swedish Suppliers

Almedahls
516 80 Dalsjöfors,
SWEDEN
Tel: 46-33-27 10 10

Charisma
Vikstensvägen 20
121 55 Johanneshov
(Kärrtorp), SWEDEN
Tel: 46-8-39 19 13

Garnstudio
Vasaplatsen 4
41134 Göteborg,
SWEDEN
Tel: 46-31-711 74 00

Ingen Konst
Palmérsvägen 9
163 46 Spånga,
SWEDEN
Tel: 46-8-761 69 70

Järbo Garn
Yllefabriksvägen 34
811 95 Järbo, SWEDEN
Tel: 46-290-706 30

Klippans Yllefabrik
Box 3
264 21 Klippan, SWEDEN
Tel: 46-435-121 35

Naturgarn
Box 16036
103 21 Stockholm,
SWEDEN
Tel: 46-8-653 28 20

Wincent
Nortullsgatan 65
113 45 Stockholm,
SWEDEN
Tel: 46-8-33 70 60

Yllet
S:t Hansgatan 19
621 56 Visby, SWEDEN
Tel: 46-498-21 40 44

List of Knot and Plaiting patterns

Key to chart symbols

1. Stockinette stitch, knit on right side, purl on wrong side

2. Reverse stockinette, purl on right side and knit on wrong side

3. knit st knitted on both sides. Selvage stitch.

4. Increase sign: Increase 1 knit stitch to right (See The New Technique, pp 112-113).

5. Increase 1 knit stitch to left (See The New Technique, pp 112-113).

6. Number of increased stitches (not part of Viking pattern). The number tells how many stitches to knit into the base stitch.

7. Knit 2 together on right side of work or purl 2 together on wrong side of work.

8. PSSO or SSK decrease on right side of work, or purl 2 twisted together on wrong side.

9. Purl 2 twisted together on right side of work, or PSSO (or SSK) on wrong side of work.

10. P 2 together on right side of work or k 2 together on wrong side.

11. Skip over this: no stitch knitted here. Included only to simplify reading the chart above it.

12. Cross 2 knit stitches over 2 knit stitches, to right.

13. Cross 2 knit stitches over 2 knit stitches, to left.

14. Cross 2 knit stitches over 2 purl stitches, to right

15. Cross 2 knit stitches over 2 purl stitches, to left

16. Cross 2 knit stitches over 1 purl stitch, to right

17. Cross 2 knit stitches over 1 purl stitch, to left

18. Shows a turn at end of short row.